GU00356774

Welcome to London!

This opening fold-out contains a general map of London to help you visualise the ten districts discussed in this guide and four pages of valuable information, handy tips, and useful addresses.

Discover London through ten districts and ten maps

For each district there is a double-page of addresses (restaurants – listed in ascending order of price – cafés, bars, tearooms, music venues, and shops), followed by a fold-out map for the relevant area with the essential places to see (indicated on the map by a star ★). These places are by no means all that London has to offer, but to us they are unmissable. The grid-referencing system (**A** B2) makes it easy for you to pinpoint addresses quickly on the map.

Transportation and hotels in London

The last fold-out consists of a transportation map and four pages of practical information that include a selection of hotels.

Index

Lists the street names, monuments, and places to visit mentioned in this guide.

MEASUREMENTS

- 1 pound = 453 grams
- 1 pint = 0.57 liter
- 1 inch = 2.54 cm
- 1 foot = 30.48 cm
- 1 mile = 1.609 km

To convert Fahrenheit to Centigrade, subtract 32, multiply by 5, divide by 9. Thus 80F becomes 26C.

SIZES: UK/US/EUR

Women's clothes
10=8=38   12=10=40
14=12=42   16=14=44
Women's shoes
4=7½=37   5=8½=38
6=9½=39   7=10½=40
Men's shoes
8=8½=41   10=10½=43
12=12½=45

ROYAL GUARDS

LLOYD'S BUILDING

A LONDON ICON

cultural heritage.
Oct–Nov
London Film Festival
→ *Third week in Oct*
International film festival at the BFI (**H** B2).
Lord Mayor's Show
Procession for the election of the Lord Mayor.
Dec
Christmas tree and lights
→ *End Nov–early Jan*
In Trafalgar Square.

BUDGET

London is a very expensive city to live in.
Accommodation
A basic double room in the city center: £80 (with bathroom), £55 (without).
Eating out
A main course in a standard restaurant: £12–15. Fish & chips: £6–7.
Sightseeing
Entry to a museum: £6; to attractions and major sites £15–20.

Going out
A beer: £3; a cocktail: £7–10; movie theater: £9–10; entry to a club: £8–12.
London for less
International student card
Discounted entry to sights, shows, etc...
London Pass
→ *£38–82 for one to six days*
www.londonpass.com
Free entry to 55 sites and discounts in some theaters, restaurants, etc.
TKTS (**B** C4)
→ *Leicester Sq.; www.official londontheatre.co.uk/tkts*
Half-price seats for same day plays and musicals.
www.londonforfree.net
Things to do in the capital for very little money.
National museums
Most of them are free.
www.24hourmuseum.org.uk

OPENING HOURS

Museums
→ *Usually 10am–6pm (incl. Sun and bank holidays)*
Parks
→ *Dawn to dusk;*
www.royalparks.gov.uk
Restaurants
→ *Usually noon–3pm, 6.30–10.30pm (last orders)*
Pubs
→ *Usually 11am–11pm (10.30pm Sun)*
Nightclubs
→ *Most close around 3am (6am at the weekend)*
Shops
→ *Usually Mon-Sat 9/10am–6pm (later on Thu); also often open Sun noon–5 or 6pm*
Open 24/7
Restaurants, bars
Tinseltown (**D** E3)
→ *44-46 St John St, EC1*
American-style diner with a milkshake bar.
Bar Italia (**B** B3)
→ *22 Frith St, W1*
Non-alcoholic drinks, snacks, and great coffee.
Beigel Bakery (**J** A1)
→ *159 Brick Lane, E1*
An institution.

ARCHITECTURE

Gothic style
Between the 12th and 15th centuries, increasing use of sculpture and stained glass, for a more 'ornate' Gothic; **Westminster Abbey** (**A** D3)
Tudor style
(1485–1603) High fan vaulting for churches, red brick and surbased arches or Flemish-style stud work for private residences; **Lady Chapel, Westminster Abbey** (**A** D3).
Baroque (17th–18th c.) This period, marked by the Great Fire of 1666, is dominated by a restrained Baroque, despite a richness of details, especially in Wren's work; **St Paul's Cathedral** (**C** B3).
The kings George style (1714–1830) Symmetrical buildings with noble façades and colonnades inspired by Antiquity; **Belgrave Square** (**G** E1).
Victorian era
Between 1837 and 1901, it is farewell to white Georgian stone with the Gothic Revival and a return to red-brick houses; **Houses of Parliament** (**A** D3). During the industrial era, huge metallic structures sprung up everywhere; **Leadenhall Market** (**C** E3).
Contemporary London
Rebuilding of the city after the Blitz using mainly concrete. The 1980s see financial buildings being erected. The 21st century projects favor a high-tech style of glass and steel; **Swiss Re Tower** (**C** E3).

CITY PROFILE

- 33 boroughs in Greater London, 13 in Inner London
- 609 square miles
- 7.5 million inhabitants
- 28 million visitors every year
- The Thames flows 40 miles through the city

GETTING AROUND

London's boroughs are divided into districts identified by postcodes (EC = East Central, N = North, SW = South West etc) ■ As a rule, the higher the number of the district, the further it is from the city center.

GREATER LONDON

WWW.

London's official website:
→ visitlondon.com
Up-to-date tourist info; addresses of restaurants bars, movie theaters, pubs:
→ londontown.com
→ viewlondon.co.uk

TOURIST INFO

Britain and London Visitor Centre (BLVC)
→ 1 Regent St, SW1
Tel. 0870 156 6366 ; Daily 9am (9.30am Mon)–6.30pm; Sat-Sun 10am–4pm; www.visitbritain.com

TELEPHONE

USA to London
→ 011 + 44 (UK) + number, omitting the initial 0
London to the USA
→ 00 + 1 (USA) + number
Within London
→ 020 + eight-digit number starting with 7 or 8

Useful numbers
Police, fire, ambulance
→ Tel. 999 or 112
Directory enquiries
→ 118500; 118118
Operator
→ 100 national
→ 155 international
Lost Property (F B2)
→ 200 Baker St, NW1
Tel. 0845 330 9882
Mon-Fri 8.30am–4pm

DIARY OF EVENTS

Public holidays
→ Jan 1 (New Year's Day); Good Friday; Easter Monday; first Mon in May (Labor Day); last Mon in May (spring day) and in Aug (Summer day); Dec 25 (Christmas); Dec 26 (Boxing Day)
Jan-Feb
New Year's Eve Parade
→ Jan 1
Mime Festival
→ Ten days mid- to end Jan
Chinese New Year
→ End Jan-Beg Feb

in Chinatown, Soho (**B** C4).
Great Spitalfields Pancake Race
→ Shrove Tuesday; 1 pm, Tower Hill Terrace (**C** F4)
Participants run along flipping pancakes in a pan.
March
St Patrick's Day
→ March 17
Party time in London's many Irish pubs.
The Boat Race
→ End March,
Held on the Thames: Oxford University vs Cambridge University.
April-May
London Marathon
→ Third Sun
Chelsea Flower Show
→ Third or fourth week
At the Royal Hospital (**G** E3).
June
Trooping the Colour
→ Second Sat
The Queen's Birthday;
Derby Day, Royal Ascot
→ Early June
Famous horse races.

July-Aug
Wimbledon
→ End June-beg July
One of the four Grand Slam's tournaments.
Proms
→ Mid-July-mid-Sep
Classical music concerts at the Royal Albert Hall (**F** F4).
Notting Hill Carnival (F B2)
→ Last weekend in Aug
Impressive Caribbean street festival.
Coin Street Festival (H C2)
→ Three weeks in summer
Cultural events in the open air.
Sep
Thames Festival
→ Second weekend
Celebration of London's river with open-air events, street theater, fireworks.
Riverfront Jazz Festival
→ Ten days end of month
In Greenwich (**J**).
London Open House
→ Third weekend
The chance to explore London's rich and varied

Welcome to London!

HAMPSTEAD HEATH

CRICKLEWOOD LA.
A5
A407
HENDON WAY
EDGWARE ROAD
WILLESDEN LANE

D KENTISH TOWN

HAMPSTEAD

A501

KENTISH TOWN RD

BROADWAY

ST JOHN'S WOOD

A5205

PRIMROSE HILL

CAMDEN TOWN

CAMDEN MARKET

SHOOT UP HILL

E
WELLINGTON HOSPITAL

REGENT'S PARK

ST PANCRAS INTERNATIONAL

EUSTON STATION

B

HARROW ROAD

MAIDA VALE

LITTLE VENICE

WESTWAY

MARYLEBONE

WALLACE COLLECTION

WEST END

BRITISH MUSEUM

F PADDINGTON

PORTOBELLO ROAD MARKET

PADDINGTON STATION

OXFORD STREET

MAYFAIR

SOHO

BAYSWATER

A40

NOTTING HILL

BAYSWATER ROAD

KENSINGTON GARDENS

HYDE PARK

A
GREEN PARK

A4

ST JAMES'S PARK

HOLLAND PARK

KENSINGTON PALACE

SERPENTINE

KNIGHTSBRIDGE

BUCKINGHAM PALACE

KENSINGTON

ROYAL ALBERT HALL

V&A MUSEUM

BELGRAVE SQUARE

WESTMINSTER

NATURAL HISTORY MUSEUM

VICTORIA STATION

TATE BRITAIN

SOUTH KENSINGTON

A4

EARL'S COURT

PIMLICO

HAMMERSMITH

WEST BROMPTON

CHELSEA

FULHAM

BATTERSEA PARK

BATTERSEA PARK ROAD

G

FULHAM PALACE RD

A308

FULHAM RD

A217

R. THAMES

BATTERSEA

A3036

HURLINGHAM PARK

PUTNEY HIGH ST

TRINITY ROAD

ST JOHN'S HILL

CLAPHAM

CLAPHAM COMMON LONG ROAD

CLAPHAM COMMON

CAVENDISH ROAD

0   1   2 km
1/ 100 000 - 1 cm = 1 km

Trafalgar Square opens out onto two imposing avenues, the Mall and Whitehall, both lined with prominent symbols of political and religious power: the royal residence, ministries, churches and the seat of government at Westminster. Once past Victoria Tower Gardens, narrow streets bordered by 18th-century façades wind their way around Smith Square. Further south, residential districts built mainly in the Victorian period radiate a tranquil atmosphere which gradually evaporates the closer you get to Victoria Station.

Set menu prices exclude drinks and service. The prices of dishes are average prices for a main course only.

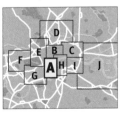

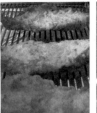

SEAFRESH

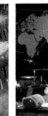

INSTITUTE OF CONTEMPORAR

RESTAURANTS

Seafresh (**A** A5)
→ 80-81 Wilton Rd, SW1
Tel. 020 7828 0747; Mon-Fri
noon–3pm, 7–10.30pm;
Sat noon–10.30pm
Enormous servings of fish (fried or grilled) and chips and excellent soups in this very popular, gaily-decorated restaurant. Dishes £11.

Matsuri (**A** B1)
→ 15 Bury St, SW1; Tel. 020 7839 1101; Daily noon–2.30pm, 6–10.30pm
Japanese cuisine raised to an art form, with sublime sushi and sashimi and impeccable service. Teppanyaki downstairs, where chefs show off their knife skills. Menus £17 (lunch)–48.

Al Duca (**A** B1)
→ 4-5 Duke of York St, SW1
Tel. 020 7839 3090
Mon-Sat noon–2.30pm,
(3pm Sat), 6–11pm
Excellent Italian cuisine in a dining room soberly decorated in sandy yellows and brick reds. Set menus £22 (lunch)–32.

Inn the Park (**A** C2)
→ St James's Park, SW1
Tel. 020 7451 9999; Daily 8 (9am Sat-Sun)–11am, noon–8.30pm (last booking)
Set in one of London's best locations, at the heart of St James's Park, overlooking the lake, Oliver Peyton's stylish, curvy, wood-and-glass restaurant serves up an equally stylish English cuisine, with a strong emphasis on local, specialist suppliers: corn fed Suffolk chicken, Shetland organic salmon Herdwick lamb, Cornish halibut. Menus £25–29.5

The National Dining Rooms (**A** C1)
→ Trafalgar Square,
Sainsbury Wing, WC2
Tel. 020 7747 2525; Daily
10am–5pm (8pm Wed)
The team efforts of, again restauranteur Oliver Peyt and über-designer David Collins (also responsible for the National Café, at t eastern side of the galler this sleek and comfortab restaurant in the Nationa Gallery has Renaissance-style frescoes, oak floorin leather seats and views o Trafalgar Square from a fe banquettes. Modern Briti fare and classic comfort food for breakfast, lunch afternoon tea.
Menus £23-28.

The Wolseley (**A** B1)
→ 160 Piccadilly, W1
Tel. 020 7499 6996
Mon-Sat 7am–midnight
(9am Sat); Sun 9am–11pm
The brainchild of three m

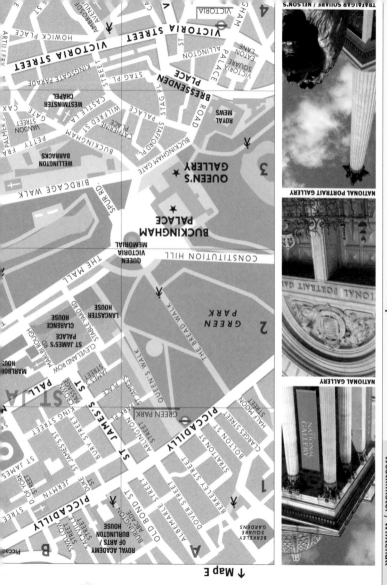

TRAFALGAR SQUARE / NELSON'S...

NATIONAL PORTRAIT GALLERY

NATIONAL GALLERY

HORSE GUARDS

BUCKINGHAM PALACE

★ **National Gallery** (A C1)
→ *Trafalgar Square, WC2*
Tel. 020 7747 2885
Daily 10am–6pm (9pm Wed)
www.nationalgallery.org.uk
Founded in 1824 with the acquisition of 38 pictures from the banker John Julius Angerstein, the National Gallery houses one of the world's best collections of European painting from the 13th to the 20th centuries. The most famous pieces include the *Pentecost* by Giotto, *Pope Julius II* by Raphael, *The Ambassadors* by Holbein, the *Sunflowers* by Van Gogh and *A Young Woman Standing at a Virginal* by Vermeer. Excellent talks and daily events.

★ **National Portrait Gallery** (A C1)
→ *St Martin's Place, WC2*
Tel. 020 7306 0055; Daily
10am–6pm (9pm Thu-Fri)
A wonderful history of England in pictures, with more than 9,000 portraits (paintings, etchings, drawings and photographs) of statesmen, musicians, writers and artists, from Nicholas Hilliard's portrait of Elizabeth I in 1572, to the portrait of Diana, Princess of Wales by David Bailey.

★ **Trafalgar Square / Nelson's Column** (A C1)
A focal point for tourists, and the geographical center of the capital. In 2003 the north of the square was

pedestrianized, and a grand staircase was built to link the now traffic-free area, in front of the National Gallery, with the square below. At its center is the 185-foot-high column dedicated to the British naval hero Admiral Nelson. The bas-reliefs on the base were made of bronze from cannons seized during Nelson's victories over the French and Spanish fleets at the Battle of Trafalgar in 1805.

★ **Horse Guards** (A D2)
→ *Whitehall, SW1*
Changing of the Guards daily
11am (10am Sun)
Four imperturbable guards mounted on superb horses

and wearing distinctiv bearskin hats are po on guard in front of t barracks of the Roya The esplanade on th of St James's Park is best vantage point.

★ **Buckingham Palace** (A A3)
→ *The Mall, SW1; Tel. c*
7766 7300; Aug-Sep: 9
3.45pm; www.royal.go
This palace has beer home of the British monarchy since Que Victoria took up resic here in 1837. It is onl to visitors in the sum but the Changing of I Guards draws crowds year round. Look out raised flag: it means

TOWER BRIDGE AS SEEN FROM QUEEN'S WALK

PUBS

Former regulations restricting pubs' opening hours are being liberalized but for most, the bell still rings at 10.50pm, the time for last orders.

Gastropubs

Boundaries between bar, pub and restaurant have been blurred since 1991, when a genuine old British pub bought by two friends started to produce very good, simple food at reasonable prices. Thus The Eagle (Farringdon Rd, **C** A1) became the first 'gastropub', a term today synonymous with quality food in relaxed surroundings.

ngt-Quatre (G B3)
325 Fulham Rd, SW3
posh diner for delicious acks and breakfasts.

narmacy
afash (G A3)
233 Old Brompton Rd, SW5
l. 0207373 2798

ATING OUT

e variety of food offered d the creativity of any British and foreign efs working in London ake the capital an tstanding place to eat – money is no object. ine is often what makes e bill soar.

alue for money
e-theater menu
reasonably-priced set enu in the early part of e evening.

bs and gastropubs
rst-rate meals at pleasant ices. The food is more aborate in gastropubs.
sh & chips / Pie & mash

Two substantial meals for just a few pounds. Pie & mash with jellied eels; fish & chips: fish deep-fried in batter, with chunky chips.

Tipping

A 12.5 percent charge is usually automatically added to the bill. If it isn't and you're happy with the service, leave some cash. If it is, you do not have to leave a further tip. You do not even have to pay for it if the service was really bad.
Note Many of London's gastronomic restaurants operate two services a night, whereby you book a table for 7–9pm or for 9pm until closing time. Sadly, you may often feel rushed if you have booked the earlier slot.

GOING OUT

Nightlife

London is unrivaled as a venue for hearing the latest

sounds, with a tradition of rock that is streets ahead of any other city. Soho, Notting Hill, and Camden have a dynamic nightlife, but in the last few years the East End has been catching up with them.
Nightspots
As well as its famous clubs, there are many bars and pubs with dance floors or spaces for live music. There usually is an admission charge, bouncers and strict controls.

Shows
Ticket Master
→ *173 Arlington Rd, Camden www.ticketmaster.co.uk*
Also
→ *www.lastminute.com*

SHOPPING

London offers a hugely varied choice for shoppers, from the luxury delights of Bond Street to the second-hand bargains in suburban

high streets.
Fashion
Everything from second-hand bargains to the heights of price and style, but the vintage clothes shops and cutting-edge designers stand out.
What, where...
Department stores on Oxford and Regent's St (**B**), *streetwear* in Soho (**B**), chic around Brompton Rd and on King's Rd (**G**), Gothic around Camden (**D**) or avant-garde in Hoxton (**C**) and on Brick Lane (**J**).
Record stores
There are many second-hand CD stores in Soho, Camden and Notting Hill.

MARKETS

Clothes, bric-à-brac, second-hand
Brick Lane (**C** F1)
→ *Around Brick Lane;*
Sun 8am–2pm
Petticoat Lane's less

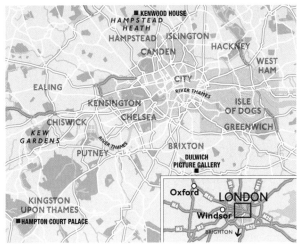

EXCURSIONS

EXCURSIONS

Hampstead Heath and Kenwood House
→ *Highgate subway station (Northern line)*
This stunning Georgian house (now a museum) overlooks the city from the top of Hampstead Heath, London's largest parkland.

Kew Gardens
→ *Kew Rd; Kew Gardens subway station (District line)*
A wonderful 19th-century park and a UNESCO site. Japanese garden, greenhouses and all varieties of flowers and trees.

Hampton Court Palace
→ *East Molesey, Surrey; Hampton Court rail station, 36 mins by train from Waterloo (**H** C3)*
The palace of Henry VIII. Don't miss the Tudor kitchens and the world-famous maze.

Royal Observatory
→ *Greenwich Park; Cutty Sark station with Docklands Light Railway*
This observatory, built by Wren, is cut in half by the Greenwich meridian.

Dulwich Picture Gallery
→ *Gallery Rd, Dulwich Village; West Dulwich station, Orpington Line;*
One of the most outstanding collections of European old masters (Poussin to Rembrandt).

Brighton
→ *50 minutes by train from Victoria station (**A** A4)*
Londoners' seaside destination.

Oxford
→ *90 mins by train from Paddington station (**F** F1)*
The most famous university town.

crowded but slightly more expensive rival. Go early.
Petticoat Lane (C E3)
→ *Middlesex St; Mon-Fri 8am–4pm; Sun 9am–2pm*
London's oldest street market, half-way between antique and second-hand.

Flowers
Columbia Road (J A1)
→ *Columbia Rd; Sun 8am–2pm*
The prettiest market, for keen gardeners.

Food
Food Lovers (B D4)
→ *Covent Garden Second Fri of the month*
Farmers' market.
Borough Market
→ *See* **I**

SEEING LONDON

By bus
City buses
Pass by London's main monuments for the price of a bus ticket with nos 11 (Victoria–Liverpool St)

and 15 (Marble Arch–Tower Bridge).
London Duck Tours
→ *020 7928 3132 www.londonducktours.co.uk*
This amphibious duck-shaped bus ends its journey in the Thames.
By boat
London River Service
→ *Tel. 020 7222 1234 www.tfl.gov.uk/river*
Boat trips on the Thames.
Jason's Trip
→ *Tel. 020 7286 3428 www.jasons.co.uk*
Down the canal from Little Venice to Camden.
Tate to Tate
→ *Tel. 020 7887 8888 £4 per journey*
Tate Britain to Tate Modern (or vice-versa) by boat, passing by the London Eye.
On foot
The Original London Walks
→ *Tel. 020 7624 3978 www.walks.com*
Over 100 guided group walks every week.

SPORTS

Lords (E A2)
→ *St John's Wood Rd, NW8*
Tel. 020 7289 1611
The cricket pitch hosting the finals of the most important test matches.
Epsom Downs
→ *Epsom (Surrey)*
Tel. 01372 470 047; From London Waterloo Station
Londoners' favorite horse-racing course in the county of Surrey (the Oaks and the Derby are held in June).
Twickenham
→ *Whitton Rd, Twickenham; District subway line, stop at Richmond rail station*
Tel. 0874 052000
The stronghold of rugby. Six Nations rugby matches are played (Jan to March).
Wimbledon Stadium
→ *Plough Lane; subway station: Tooting Broadway*
Tel. 0870 840 8905
Greyhound races (Tue, Fri-Sat nights).

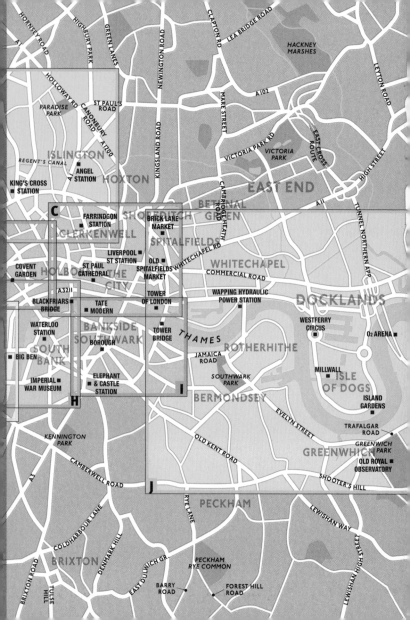

'NUM & MASON

JERMYN STREET

BURLINGTON ARCADE

already responsible for such enduringly successful London restaurants as The Ivy and J. Sheekey, the Wolseley is a splendid, high-ceilinged 1920s building which looks like a Viennese brasserie, with gold-and-black decor and a chequerboard marble floor. Impeccable brasserie-type food. Book ahead. Dishes £12–25.

CAFÉ, BARS, CLUB, CULTURAL CENTER

Tiles (A A4)
→ 36 Buckingham Palace Rd SW1; Tel. 020 7834 7761
Mon-Fri noon–11pm
A wonderfully cozy wine bar across from Victoria Station, with a warm decor and plush sofas in the basement, where the atmosphere is slightly more jazzy. Simple, pleasantly-priced dishes are available (fish cakes, risotto, mezes, etc.).

Cinnamon Club (A C4)
→ The Old Westminster Library, Great Smith St, SW1
Library Bar open from 10am;
Club Bar: Mon-Sat
6–11.45pm
This striking, now listed, former library building houses one of London's best Indian restaurants

and two bars. In the old Reading Room is the Library Bar, with a hushed atmosphere to the taste of politicians from the nearby Parliament who often come here. The cocktail bar is down the marble stairs, and a strikingly different setting – modern and cooler. Long list of bellinis (try the cinnamon one), lassis, and martinis. Bar food as well.

Tiger Tiger (A C1)
→ 29 Haymarket, SW1
Mon-Sat noon–3am;
Sun 2pm–midnight
With three levels, five bars, two dance floors, a club and a restaurant, Tiger Tiger should keep you amused for a while. A quiet place to hang out during the day, it gets more vibrant, busy and noisy as night closes in.

Institute of Contemporary Arts (A C2)
→ The Mall, SW1
Daily noon–1am (10.30pm Sun-Mon); www.ica.org.uk
An amazing multicultural space, half gallery, half movie theater, showing underground films or little-known classics. It also organizes lectures, exhibitions, club nights, and has a great bar too.

SHOPPING

Dover Street Market (A A1)
→ 17-18 Dover St, W1
Tel. 020 7518 0680
Mon-Sat 11am–6pm
(7pm Thu)
A fascinating store run by Comme des Garçons designer Rei Kawakubo and her husband, and a must for anyone seriously interested in contemporary fashion; dresses, jewelry, shoes, bags over five floors by Carla Sozzani, Tom Binns, Martin Margiela, Hussein Chalayan, and others.

Fortnum & Mason (A B1)
→ 181 Piccadilly W1
Mon-Sat 10am–10pm;
Sun noon–6pm
The legendary, ornate 300-year-old food hall is full to overflowing with teas, shortbreads, marmalades, chutneys and other exquisite, and expensive, fare. Tearoom at the back of the store.

Jermyn Street (A B1)
Famous street with mostly men's shops.
Davidoff of London (no. 35) Cigars.
Turnbull & Asser (no. 71) Bespoke shirtmaker.
John Lobb (no. 88) Shoes.

Floris (no. 89) Founded in 1730, it sells a beautiful range of soaps and fragrances.

Burlington Arcade (A A1)
→ Mon-Sat 8am–6.30pm
Built in 1819 for Lord George Cavendish, the Regency-style gallery was Britain's first shopping mall. The Beadles, in their Edwardian uniforms and top hats, still guard the entrance to the arcade and its luxury boutiques selling jewelry, shoes, cashmere, and perfumes.

Waterstone's (A B1)
→ 203-206 Piccadilly, W1
Tel. 020 7851 2400; Mon-Sat
10am–10pm; Sun noon–6pm
A huge bookstore, with more than one million books in stock and comfy chairs to read them in. The fifth-floor View Bar & Food affords views of the Houses of Parliament.

Hatchards (A B1)
→ 187 Piccadilly, W1
Tel. 020 7439 9921; Mon-Sat
9am–6pm; Sun noon–6pm
You may, however, find more pleasure in browsing a few doors down, in London's oldest bookstore. Founded in 1797 by John Hatchard, it is full of character, with soft carpets and a grand creaking wooden staircase.

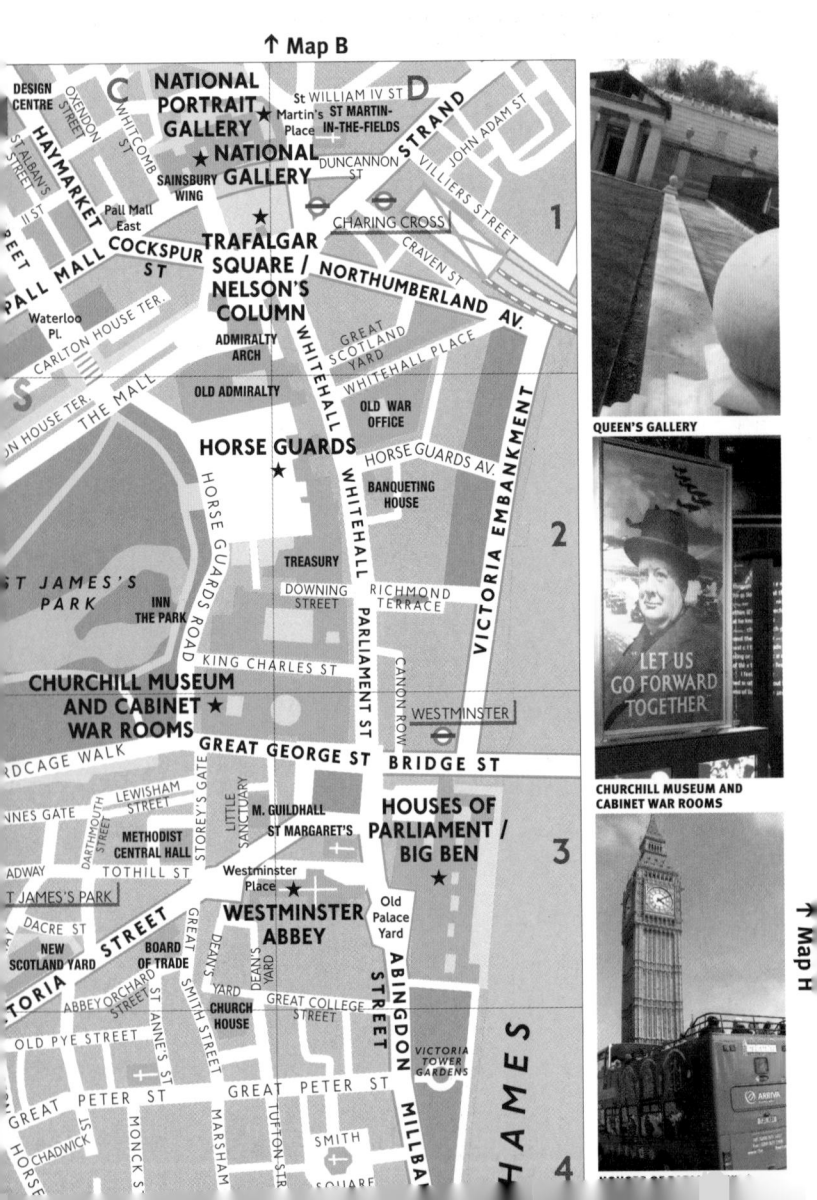

↑ Map B

QUEEN'S GALLERY

CHURCHILL MUSEUM AND CABINET WAR ROOMS

↑ Map H

WESTMINSTER ABBEY

TATE BRITAIN

...een is at home. Close ...s Clarence House, the ...don home of the Queen ...her until her death in ...2, now the London ...dence of her grandson, ...ce Charles, and his wife, ...Duchess of Cornwall. ...house is partly open to ...public in the summer ...ts must be pre-booked).

...Queen's Gallery (A A3)
➜ *...uckingham Palace Rd*
...020 7766 7301
...y 10am–5.30pm
...Queen's Gallery, on the ...t front of Buckingham ...ce, was built in 1962 ...of the bomb-damaged ...s of the former private ...pel. It displays a ...nging selection from

the royal collection's 9,000 paintings – one of the richest private collections in the world.

★ **Churchill Museum and Cabinet War Rooms (A** C3)
➜ *Clive Steps, King Charles St, SW1; Tel. 020 7930 6961*
Daily 9.30am–6pm
These reinforced chambers played a crucial role in history as Churchill's HQ during World War Two. Faithful reconstruction of life in the underground complex, and interactive 50-ft long lifeline charting Churchill's life.

★ **Houses of Parliament / Big Ben (A** D3)
➜ *Westminster Place, SW1*
Tel. 0870 906 3773 (by appt)

The 13-ton bell known as Big Ben chimes the hours and quarters. The neo-Gothic architecture of the houses was designed by Charles Barry and Augustus Pugin after fire destroyed the previous building in 1834. You can sit in on debates between Oct-July.

★ **Westminster Abbey (A** D3)
➜ *Dean's Yard, SW1*
Mon-Sat 9.30am– 4.45pm
(7pm Wed; 2.45pm Sat)
The finest religious building in London, a masterpiece of flamboyant Gothic. Coronations have taken place here beneath the high ribbed vaulting since 1308: the actual Coronation Chair

used in the ceremony is on view in one of the chapels. Many famous people are buried in the abbey or have a statue to mark their passing. The most celebrated tomb of all is that of King Edward the Confessor (1042–66).

★ **Tate Britain (A** D5)
➜ *Millbank SW1*
Tel. 020 7887 8008; Daily 10am–5.50pm
Tate Britain is devoted solely to English art from 1500 to the present day. The works are arranged thematically, with some rooms dedicated to individual major British artists. The adjacent Clore Gallery still houses the marvelous Turner collection.

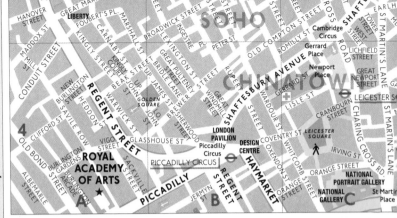

LONDON TRANSPORT MUSEUM

SOMERSET HOUSE

★ **British Museum** (**B** C2)
→ *Great Russell St, WC1
Mon-Sat 10am–5.30pm
(8.30pm Thu-Fri)*
In 1753, Hans Sloane, a physician, naturalist and traveler, bequeathed his collection of curios to the nation. This formed the nucleus of the museum, which now has one of the world's greatest collections of antiquities and ethnographic works (more than 6 million exhibits), including the Rosetta Stone and the Parthenon frieze, which is causing much controversy. In 1997 the spaces vacated by the British Library (which went to Euston) were redesigned

by Norman Foster. The magnificent Reading Room is now open to the public.
★ **Sir John Soane's Museum** (**B** E3)
→ *13 Lincoln's Inn Fields, WC2
Tel. 020 7405 2107; Tue-Sat
10am–5pm; candlelit visit first
Tue of the month 6–9pm*
The renowned architect, art lover and eccentric, John Soane, transformed his home into a remarkable museum during his lifetime. Well-placed mirrors and sliding panels reveal an amazing collection of books, antiquities and paintings.
★ **Royal Opera House** (**B** D3)
→ *Bow St, WC2; Tel. 020 7304

4000; Tours by reservation
Mon-Fri: 10.30am, 12.30pm,
2.30pm; Sat: 10.30am,
11.30am, 12.30pm, 1.30pm*
The most prestigious opera house in the city, better known as 'Covent Garden', is now graced by a monumental glass window, built using the existing basic structure designed by Edmund M. Barry in 1858.
★ **Covent Garden** (**B** D4)
The vegetable garden of the convent attached to Westminster Abbey and the early fruit and vegetable market which used to stand here have disappeared, but the square designed by Inigo Jones (1631) remains very popular – and touristy.

The pretty arched galle▮
(1832), the iron and gla▮
market halls and the ar▮
around are home to a multitude of stores, cra▮
stalls, cafés, restauran▮
and street entertainers.
★ **London Transport Museum** (**B** D4)
→ *Covent Garden Piazza,
Tel. 020 7565 7299
Mon-Thu, Sat-Sun 10am–
6pm; Fri 11am–9pm*
Located in one of Cove▮
Garden's former floral ▮
(1871), one of London's most entertaining mus▮
finally reopened in 20▮
bigger than ever before▮
★ **Somerset House** (**B** E4)
→ *Strand, WC2; Tel. 020*

OXFORD CIRCUS

OXFORD STREET

TOTTENHAM COURT ROAD

ST GILES HIGH ST

ST PATRICK

SOHO

NEW OXFORD

GREAT RUSSELL

BLOOMSBURY

BEDFORD AVE

BAINBRIDGE ST

STREATHAM ST

BEDFORD SQUARE

ADELINE PLACE

MONTAGUE PLACE

BRITISH MUSEUM

IMAGINATION OFFICES AND GALLERY

BALLET GALLERY

STORE STREET

MORWELL STREET

HANWAY PLACE

CRESS STREET

RATHBONE PLACE

PERCY ST

WINDMILL ST

RATHBONE STREET

NEWMAN STREET

BERNERS MEWS BERNERS PL.

BERNERS STREET

EASTCASTLE STREET

WINSLEY STREET

MARGARET ST

WELLS STREET

MORTIMER STREET

RIDING HOUSE STREET

GREAT TITCHFIELD ST

PORTLAND ST

REGEN

MIDDLESEX HOSPITAL

FITZROVIA

TOY MUSEUM

GOODGE ST

CHENIES STREET

TOTTENHAM STREET

CHARLOTTE STREET

GOODGE STREET

HOWLAND STREET

MAPLE STREET

CLEVELAND STREET

LANGHAM ST

FOLEY STREET

GOSFIELD STREET

CAVENDISH ST

NEW CAVENDISH STREET

CLIPSTONE ST

GREAT TITCHFIELD STREET

ROYAL EAR HOSPITAL

LONDON TELECOM TOWER

LONDON FOOT HOSPITAL

UNIVERSITY OF LONDON

GOWER STREET

MALET STREET

RIDGMOUNT STREET

RIDGMOUNT GARDENS

TORRINGTON PLACE

CHENIES MEWS

HUNTLEY STREET

WHITFIELD STREET

FITZROY STREET

GRAFTON WAY

WARREN STREET

FITZROY SQUARE

WARREN ST

SCHOOL OF ORIENTAL AND AFRICAN STUDIES

TORRINGTON SQUARE

THORNHAUGH STREET

UNIV. COLL. HOSPITAL

NAT. CENTRAL LIBRARY

CHURCH OF CHRIST

UNIVERSITY COLLEGE

UNIVERSITY STREET

GORDON SQUARE

GORDON STREET

WOBURN SQUARE

BEDFORD WAY

WOBURN PL

TAVISTOCK

RUSSELL S

TAVISTOCK SQUARE

ENDSLEIGH PL

GORDON SQ

TAVITON ST

ENDSLEIGH STREET

ENDSLEIGH GARDENS

GORDON ST

EUSTON SQUARE

GOWER PLACE

EUSTON SQUARE

EUSTON ROAD

NORTH GOWER STREET

HAMPSTEAD RD

DRUMMOND ST

STANHOPE STREET

TRITON SQUARE

WELLCOME MEDICAL MUSEUM

BRITISH ASS.

UPPER WOBURN PLACE

Cartwr Garden

1 2 A B C

SIR JOHN SOANE'S MUSEUM

BRITISH MUSEUM

BRITISH MUSEUM

There is never a quiet moment in the area between Oxford Circus and Covent Garden. By day the mood is set by the bustling shoppers along Regent Street and the often unbearably jam-packed Oxford Street (best avoided on Saturdays), and by hungry tourists strolling through Chinatown or sitting at the café-terraces of Covent Garden. In the evening the theaters are invaded by devotees of plays and musicals, and cosmopolitan Soho's many restaurants, gay bars and rather tame sex shops draw teeming crowds. Further east, Holborn's law courts signify justice; to the north, Bloomsbury and its rich literary past represents knowledge, with the British Museum and UCL, University College London, as its emblems.

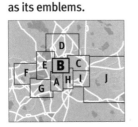

NEW WORLD

WORLD FOOD CAFÉ

RESTAURANTS

Chinatown (B B-C4)
Chinatown abounds with restaurants. Here are two we like: Harbour City at 46 Gerrard St; New World at 1 Gerrard Place.
World Food Café (B C3)
→ 14 Neal's Yard, WC2
Mon-Sat 11.30am–4.30pm
At the heart of New Age London, vegetarian cuisine with an exotic twist, to have in or take out. Dishes £5–12.
Malabar Junction (B A3)
→ 107 Great Russell St, WC1
Tel. 020 7580 5230
Daily noon–3pm, 6–11pm
Very good South Indian (Kerala) cuisine at more than reasonable prices for such a location. Friendly, unhurried service. Dishes £8–12. The lower ground Malabar Express has a set menu for £5 (noon–3pm).
Masala Zone (B A3)
→ 9 Marshall St, W1
Tel. 020 7287 9966
Sun-Fri noon–3pm, 5.30–11pm; Sat 12.30–11pm
The owners of two of the best Indian restaurants in London (see Amaya, **G**), have opened this smart canteen, where you can eat fresh and flavorsome Indian food: curries, thalis (platters with several small dishes), snacks

(masala lamb burger, chicken tikka ciabatta) and vegetarian dishes. One of the best deals in the West End. Dishes £11.
Barrafina (B B3)
→ 54 Frith St, W1; Daily noon–3pm, 5–11pm (10.30pm Sun)
The small tapas bar of brothers Sam and Eddie Hart. Always busy and with a no-booking policy so it may be hard to find a free stool – and there are only 23 available. Pricey but faultless. Tapas £5–15.
Abeno Too (B C4)
→ 17-18 Great Newport St, WC1; Tel. 020 7379 1160; Daily noon–11pm (10pm Sun)
With a hotplate in front of each diner in this Japanese canteen they watch the chef prepare okonomiyaki, a kind of pancake with a filling of your choice. Other surprises include delicious avocado pastries. Dishes £15.
Arbutus (B B3)
→ 63-64 Frith St, W1
Tel. 020 7734 4545;
Daily noon–2.30pm, 5–11pm (9.30pm Sun)
Michelin starred less than 18 months after opening, the brainchild of chef Anthony Demetre and co-owner Will Smith is still raved about. Seasonal menus for a modern British fare: lamb breast and

MB & FLAG

LONDON COLISEUM

CARNABY STREET

sweetbreads with white beans and sweet peppers, smoked eel with beetroot horseradish. The set lunch (£14 and £16) and pre-theater menus (£15.50 and £17.50) are excellent value for money.

Yauatcha (B B3)

→ 15 Broadwick St, W1
Tel. 020 7494 8888; Mon-Sat 11am–11.30pm (11pm Sun)
Hakkasan (8 Hanway Place, **B** B3), Alan Yau's previous venture, had a brilliant design by Christian Liaigre (much copied thereafter), the sexiest bar in London and memorable dim sum. Yauatcha is another dim sum paradise with a dimly-lit downstairs dining room, a decor of luminous fish tanks and a modern, hip vibe throughout. The only drawback, but a spreading one in London nowadays, is that you can only keep your table for 90 minutes. The teahouse upstairs has 150 types of tea and the most gorgeous miniature cakes. Dim sum £3–6.

TEAROOM

Momo (B A4)

→ 25 Heddon St, W1
Tel. 020 7734 4040
Daily noon–midnight
In a quiet alleyway off Regent Street, Momo

takes you to North Africa with mint tea and all kinds of delicacies; comfy cushions, rugs and copper platters. You can also have lunch or dinner but must reserve.

PUB, BAR, CLUB, MUSIC

Lamb & Flag (B C4)

→ 33 Rose St, WC2; Mon-Sat 11am–11pm (11.30pm Sat); Sun noon–10.30pm
The oldest pub in Covent Garden (1623). Popular but not very big, so on most nights people spill out onto the street. Wide choice of whiskies.

Aperitivo (B A4)

→ 41 Beak St, W1
Mon-Sat noon–11pm
Aperitivo's motto is 'To share is to enjoy'. It is an ideal meeting point after a tiring afternoon shopping in Soho. Good Italian-style tapas and good wine list.

Two Floors (B A4)

→ 3 Kingly St, W1
Mon-Sat noon–11.30pm
One of the most original bars in the West End, on two levels, sparsely decorated but sybaritically comfortable, themed with the color black at street level and with a basement tricked out in bamboo.

Good selection of wines by the glass and cocktails.

London Coliseum (B C4)

→ St Martin's Lane, WC2
Tel. 020 7632 8300; Sale of cheap seats (£10 or £15) Mon-Fri from 10am
This symbol of the West End has a magnificent blue and gold original decor (1904), with public gallery spaces and a glass-roofed Terrace Bar. All the operatic works are sung in English.

SHOPPING

Milroy's of Soho (B C3)

→ 3 Greek St, W1
Tel. 020 7437 9385; Mon-Sat 10am–8pm (7pm Sat)
A specialist whisky store with 600 brands from the world over on sale, including Port Ellen and Dallas Dhu, it is heaven for connoisseurs.

Berwick Street (B B3)

The street for small record stores: indie (Sister Ray at no. 34); second-hand (Revival Records at no. 30); electronic (Vinyl Junkies at no. 94).

Liberty (B A3)

→ 214 Regent St, W1
Mon-Sat 10am–9pm (7pm Sat); Sun noon–6pm
Begun in the 19th century as an outlet for the Arts

and Crafts movement, the famous 'Tudor House' remains a leading stockist of young designers' clothes.

Hamleys (B A4)

→ 188-196 Regent St, W1
Mon-Sat 10am (9am Sat)–8pm; Sun noon–6pm
Thousands of games and toys over seven floors and skilled demonstrations by staff. Beware of the maddening crowds of kids and their parents before Christmas.

Ray's Jazz Shop at Foyle's (B C3)

→ Foyle's, 113 Charing Cross Rd, WC2; Mon-Sat 9.30am–9pm; Sun noon–6pm
Ray's tiny shop is on the first floor of Foyle's bookstore, alongside an equally small but truly pleasant coffee shop. Very good selection of jazz CDs.

Carnaby St (B A4)

The symbol of the swinging 1960s has been given a drastic face lift with numerous shops around a pretty, two-story galleried courtyard, Kingly Court.

Around Covent Garden

Floral St (B D4) for Paul Smith, Nicole Farhi, Joseph, Maharishi; Neal St (B D3) for Carhartt, Birkenstock, and the Natural Shoe Store.

↑ Map C

SIR JOHN
SOANE'S
MUSEUM

HOLBORN

LINCOLN'S INN FIELDS

LINCOLN'S INN HALL

PUBLIC
RECORD
OFFICE

PATENT
OFFICE

WHETSTONE
PARK

HIGH HOLBORN

CHANCERY LANE

GRAY'S
INN

BLOOMSBURY WAY

BLOOMSBURY
SQUARE

RED LION
SQUARE

EAGLE STREET

PRINCETON
STREET

BEDFORD
ROW

LION ST

THEOBALD'S

HOLBORN 2

HARPUR
STREET

CONDUIT ST

MILLMAN STREET

DOUGHTY STREET

GREAT
ORMOND
STREET

ROYAL LONDON
HOMEOPATHIC HOSPITAL

QUEEN
SQUARE

THE HOSPITAL FOR
SICK CHILDREN

DICKENS
HOUSE

CORAM'S
FIELDS

BRUNSWICK
SQUARE

GUILFORD STREET

MECKLENBURGH
SQUARE

ST ANDREWS
GARDEN

ST GEORGE'S
GARDENS

GRAY'S INN ROAD

CLERKENWELL ROAD

ROSEBERY AVENUE

FARRINGDON ROAD

PINE ST

WARNER ST

EYRE ST
HILL

BACK
HILL

MOUNT PLEASANT

LAYSTALL ST

HATTON
WALL

LEATHER LANE

ST CROSS
ST

PORTPOOL LANE

BALDWIN'S GDNS

GRAY'S
INN
GARDENS

BROOKE ST

STAPLE INN

FURNIVAL ST

FETTER LANE

CURSITOR ST

BREAM'S BUILDINGS

CHANCERY LANE

KINGSWAY

SOUTHAMPTON ROW

NEW LONDON
THEATRE

PARKER
STREET

DRURY LANE

MACKLIN ST

STUKELEY ST

NEWTON ST

HIGH HOLBORN

AL OPERA HOUSE   COVENT GARDEN

Map labels

OPERA HOUSE

COVENT GARDEN

DRURY LANE THEATRE

ALDWYCH

BUSH HOUSE

ST CLEMENT DANES

STRAND

TEMPLE CHURCH

THEATRE MUSEUM

COVENT GARDEN

Covent Garden Piazza

LONDON TRANSPORT MUSEUM

STRAND

SOMERSET HOUSE

TEMPLE ★

MIDDLE TEMPLE GARDEN

INNER TEMPLE GARDEN

TEMPLE PLACE

VICTORIA EMBANKMENT

STRAND

SAVOY

VICTORIA EMBANKMENT

WATERLOO BRIDGE

RIVER THAMES

MARTIN-E-FIELDS D

0   100   200 m

4

E   F

PLE

ROYAL ACADEMY OF ARTS

ST MARTIN-IN-THE-FIELDS

6; Daily 10am–6pm; Mon 10am–2pm

iam Chambers' superb classical palace (1786), fountains playing in its rtyard, contains a cious art collection ueathed to the nation as as an exhibition space.

rtauld Gallery
collection of the ustrialist Samuel rtauld (1876–1947), anced by other ations, is best known ts Impressionist and timpressionist pictures uch artists as Pissarro, et, Cézanne, Monet, oir, Gauguin, Van Gogh, Modigliani. But here are a *Trinity* by Botticelli,

32 pictures by Rubens, several oil-paintings by Turner and gouaches by Rouault.

Embankment Galleries
Design, architecture, fashion and photographs, in the rooms which formerly housed the Gilbert Collection (now moved to the Victoria & Albert Museum **G** C2).

★ Temple (B F4)**
This district, owned by the Knights Templar from 1185–1312, is like a small enclave within the city. Two of the four Law Schools took up residence here in the 17th century. On either side of Middle Temple Lane stretches a labyrinth of little

streets, small courtyards and private gardens. This is also the site of the famous Middle Temple Hall, where Shakespeare's comedy *Twelfth Night* was premiered in 1600. Watch out for the pretty circular 12th-century church in the Inner Temple.

★ Royal Academy of Arts (B A4)**
→ Burlington Arcade, W1
Tel. 020 7300 8000
Daily 10am–6pm (10pm Fri)
The opening and complete refurbishment of the 'John Madejski' Fine Rooms, after more than 200 years, has allowed rare works by such artists as Gainsborough, Constable and Reynolds, to come out of storage.

The Summer Exhibition still draws the crowds, as do the big-name shows which run throughout the year.

★ St Martin-in-the-Fields (B C4)**
→ St Martin's Place WC2
Tel. 020 7766 1100
Mon-Sat 8am (9am Sat)–6pm; Sun 8am–7.30pm
A church has stood here since the 13th century. This one, designed by James Gibb in 1726, transformed the architectural style of English religious buildings. It is renowned for its candlelit Baroque music evenings and free lunchtime concerts.

GUILDHALL

ST PAUL'S CATHEDRAL

★ **Monument** (**C** D4)
→ *Monument St, EC3*
Tel. 020 7626 2717
Daily 9.30am–5pm
Erected to commemorate
the Great Fire (1666), this
impressive 203-foot-tall
column conceals a marble
staircase in its base
which leads to the top.

★ **Leadenhall
Market** (**C** D3)
→ *Whittington Ave, EC3*
Mon-Fri 7am–4pm
Don't miss this opulent
Victorian market hall with
cream and red metal arches
surmounted by a glass
dome of its aisles. Above it loom
the six aluminium towers
of the Lloyd's Building

complex (Richard Rogers,
1986).

★ **St Stephen
Walbrook** (**C** D3)
→ *39 Walbrook Court, EC4*
Tue-Fri 11.30am–4pm
Christopher Wren's
masterpiece, and one of
his most elaborate and
classical designs. The
architect used this church
to try out some of his
ideas for St Paul's.

★ **Swiss Re Tower** (**C** E3)
→ *30 St Mary Axe, EC3*
Pointing straight up in the
air at a busy street junction
stands one of architect
Norman Foster's most
distinctive works (2004),
and the sixth tallest
building in London, named

after the Swiss Re Company
which commissioned it. The
41-story, 591-ft-high tower is
covered with a skin of blue
and black glass lozenges
and its unusual bullet
shape has led Londoners to
give it the friendly nickname
of The Gherkin.

★ **Bank of England
Museum** (**C** D3)
→ *Bartholomew Lane, EC2*
Tel. 020 7601 5545
Mon-Fri 10am–5pm
Find out about the history
and day-to-day running of
the 'Old Lady of Thread-
needle Street', the powerful
Bank of England, which
stores the nation's gold in
its coffers. Founded in 1694
it was the first bank in the

world to issue cheques
★ **Guildhall** (**C** C3)
→ *Gresham St, EC2*
Tel. 020 7332 3700
Gallery: Mon-Sat 10am–5
Sun noon–4pm
The heart of the City's
municipal power beats
behind this remarkable
18th-century façade,
which reflects a fusion
Gothic, Greek and India
influences. Passing un-
the tierceron ribbed va
enter the great stone h
(151 x 49 ft), site of offi
ceremonies. The walls
decorated with the arr
of all the guilds that ha
elected the Lord Mayo
since 1319. The names
the mayors are inscrib

MONUMENT

ST STEPHEN WALBROOK

LEADENHALL MARKET

A   **B**   **C**

CITY

AMWELL STREET
ROSEBERY AVENUE
SPENCER STREET
THE CITY UNI.
Northampton Square
ST CLEMENT'S
DINGLEY ROAD
CENTRAL STREET
LEVER STREET
BATH STREET

MYDDELTON STREET
MYDDELTON STREET
SAINT JOHN STREET
GOSWELL ROAD
LEVER STREET
IRONMONGER ROW
RADNOR STREET

1

SKINNER ST
PERCIVAL STREET
BAGNIGGE
CYRUS ST
SEWARD STREET
BOWLING GREEN
TOFFEE PARK

EXMOUTH MARKET
SPA FIELDS GARDENS
CORPORATION ROW
COMPTON STREET
PEAR TREE ST
MITCHELL STREET
OLD

PINE ST
NORTHAMPTON ROAD
WOODBRIDGE ST
DARLINGTON ST
BASTWICK STREET
GEE STREET

BOWLING GREEN LA
SANS WALK
NORTHBURGH ST
BERRY ST
SUTTON

CLERKENWELL CLOSE
ST JAMES'S
CLERK GREEN
SEKFORDE
GREAT ST
ST LUKE'S
GARRETT STREET
WHITECROSS STREET
BANNER STREET

WARNER STREET
FARRINGDON LA
SAINT JOHN
GOSWELL ROAD
GOLDEN LANE
CHEQUER

BACK HILL
HERBAL HILL
CLERKENWELL ROAD
FANN STREET
FORTUNE STREET
DUFFERIN

HATTON WALL
TURNMILL ST
ST BARTHOLOMEW SCHOOL OF MEDICINE
ERROL ST

HATTON PLACE
BRISEET STREET
ST JOHN'S LANE
CHARTERHOUSE
BEECH STREET
CH

2

HATTON GARDEN
KIRBY ST
SAFFRON ST
CHARTERHOUSE SQUARE
BARBICAN CENTRE
SILK STREE

LEATHER LANE
ST CROSS ST
FARRINGDON
BARBICAN
DEFOE PLACE
BARBICAN

GREVILLE ST
COWCROSS STREET
ALDERSGATE STREET
ANDREWES HIGHWALK

ELY GARDEN
ELY CHAPEL
SMITHFIELD MARKET
LONG LANE
CLOTH FAIR
ST GILES CRIPPLEGATE
FORE STR

HIGH HOLBORN
CHARTERHOUSE ST
W. SMITHFIELD
West Smithfield
LITTLE BRITAIN
★ ST BARTHOLOMEW THE GREAT

HOLBORN
HOSIER LA.
★ MUSEUM OF LONDON
LONDON WA

NORWICH STREET
Holborn Circus
HOLBORN VIADUCT
SNOW HILL
SAINT BARTHOLOMEW'S HOSPITAL
LONDON WALL

NEW FETTER LANE
SAINT ANDREW
FARRINGDON
GILTSPUR ST
GENERAL POST OFFICE
GPO
ANGEL
ST MARTIN'S-LE-GRAND
KING EDWARD ST
FOSTER LANE
NOBLE ST
GRESHAM ST
WOOD ST
ALDERMANBURY
BASINGH

New Street Square
ST PAUL'S STATION
CENTRAL CRIMINAL COURT
NEWGATE STREET
★ GUILDHA
GRESHA

SHOE LANE

City / St Paul's / Shoreditch

Men and women scurry around here during the week, but by Saturday the City looks like a ghost town, and you have 48 hours to enjoy its deserted streets. Relics of the past, spared by the Great Fire of 1666 and the air raids of World War Two, offer a glimpse into the historic heart of London. The maze of streets and alleys hold some surprises as dull, uninspiring granite and concrete 1960s office blocks stand alongside old pubs, historic churches and the more recent innovative, graceful glass-and-steel constructions. Over the past 20 years, Shoreditch and the southern half of Hoxton, northeast of the City, have acquired a vibrant arts and entertainment scene. Its bars have become a magnet for night revelers.

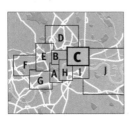

JONES DAIRY CAFÉ THE REAL GREEK SOUVLAKI

RESTAURANTS

Jones Dairy Café (C F1, J A1)
→ 23 Ezra St, E2; Fri-Sun 9am–3pm (2pm Sun)
This unusual dairy-café housed in a former stable serves only farm-sourced and organic produce such as eggs, porridge, pancakes and Colchester oysters. On Sundays it gets very busy with crowds from the nearby Columbia Road flower market.

The Place Below (C C3)
→ St Mary Le Bow, Cheapside, EC2
Mon-Fri 7.30am–3pm
Excellent vegetarian café in the Norman crypt of the church, which makes for an unusual setting. In summer, eat in or take out on one of the few tables upstairs. Dishes £7.50.

Moshi Moshi Sushi (C E3)
→ Liverpool Street Station 24 Upper Level, Broadgate
Mon-Fri 11.30am–10pm
This sushi bar, London's first kaiten (conveyor belt) when it opened in 1995, hangs above the stations platforms. Sushi £3; dishes £11.

The Real Greek Souvlaki (C A1)
→ 140 St John St, EC1
Tel. 020 7253 7234
Mon-Sat noon–11pm
Superior Greek 'street food', with lamb, pork or chicken kebabs (souvlakis) and mezes whose ingredients vary with the seasons. Modern wood and steel decor with high tables around an open kitchen. Good Greek wines. Meze £4, dishes to share £20.

St John Bread and Wine (C F2)
→ 94-96 Commercial St, E1
Tel. 020 7247 8924
Mon-Fri 9am–11pm; Sat-Sun 10am–11pm (10.30pm Sun)
Those interested in contemporary eating – and in offals in particular – will know Fergus Henderson's St John on St John Street (C B2). At this more informal spot you are offered a simpler version of the same seasonal classics: ox heart & pickled walnut, pea and ham soup, crispy Welsh pig with dandelion & mustard. Delicious homemade bread and desserts. Busy, buzzing, friendly. Dishes £15.

The Peasant (C A1)
→ 240 St John St, EC1
Tel. 020 7336 7726
Restaurant: Tue-Fri noon–3pm, 6–11pm; Sat 6–11pm; Sun noon–3pm
This atmospheric Victorian pub was, with The Eagle (159 Farringdon Rd, C A2),

RUSALEM TAVERN

A. GOLD

HOXTON BOUTIQUE

one of the forerunners of the gastropub revolution Beautiful bar with round horseshoe counter at street level and a gorgeous restaurant upstairs, with high ceilings, wide windows, a fireplace in winter, and a small terrace at the rear in summer. Delicious food: cured venison bresaola with poached pear, roast halibut and light bouillabaisse. Dishes £15.

BARS, PUBS, NIGHTCLUB

Ye Olde Mitre (C A2)
→ 1 Ely Court, via 8 Hatton Garden, EC1
Mon-Fri 11.30am–11pm
Two minutes' walk from the noise of the City, down a hidden alleyway, is this oak-fronted gem of a pub, one of London's oldest (1546). City workers love to come here for a pint after work, relishing its friendly atmosphere, and no doubt the change of scene this corner of 16th-century England provides.

Jerusalem Tavern (C A2)
→ 55 Britton St, EC1
Mon-Fri 11am–11pm
An historic pub of great charm despite its crumbling façade. The list of beers on offer includes

a few surprises such as lemon and ginger, honey, and organic beer as well. Traditional food is also available.

Cargo (C E1)
→ 83 Rivington St, EC2
Tel. 020 7749 7844
Daily 6pm–1am (3am Fri-Sat; midnight Sun)
Dub, reggae, disco, hip-hop, superstar DJs and bands, Cargo, under the arches of a railway bridge, isn't out of place in ultra-trendy Shoreditch. Down the road, at no. 62, is **Bedroom Bar**, another Hoxton favorite.

Fabric (C A2)
→ 77a Charterhouse St, EC1
Fri 9.30pm–5am;
Sat 10pm–7pm
This mythical club welcomes the best DJs in the world and the most knowledgeable of dance music-loving crowds. In one of the three rooms the 'bodysonic' floor vibrates to the frequencies of the bass speakers. Last year Fabric opened its own dream venue, Matter, under the dome of the O2 Arena (J A2).

CULTURAL CENTER

Barbican (C C2)
→ Silk St, EC2
Tel. 020 7638 8891

Daily 9am (noon Sun)–11pm
www.barbican.org.uk
Make the effort to visit this cavernous and austere maze of concrete (which, it is true, is more enjoyable when the terrace is bathed in sunshine). This is a major arts center and renowned concert hall for classical, jazz and world music, and contemporary dance. Great program of free music in the foyer.

SHOPPING

A. Gold (C F2)
→ 42 Brushfield St, E1
Tel. 020 7247 2487; *Mon-Fri 9.30am–5.30pm ; Sat-Sun 11am (10am Sun)–6pm*
British produce, made to traditional methods, sold in a shop which looks like a cottage: cakes, jams, gingerbread, bacon pies, cheeses, pickles etc.

Old Spitalfields Market (C F2)
→ Brushfield St, E1; *Mon-Fri 11am–4pm; Sun 9am–5pm;*
www.visitspitalfields.com
This much-loved old covered market, built in 1682, survived the Blitz, but couldn't resist promoters' plans for trendy new office buildings. The number of stalls selling knickknacks,

new-age products, hip and retro clothes by young talented designers, was halved but the market remains a fun destination and the area around certainly is worth a stroll.

Hoxton (C E1)
A lively district north of Shoreditch, fast becoming famous for its fashion-houses.

Relax Garden (C E1)
→ 40 Kingsland Rd, E2
Daily noon–7pm (8pm Thu-Fri; 6pm Sun)
Clothes by unknown designers at hot prices: stylish tunics, dresses, and bags.

No-One (C E1)
→ 1 Kingsland Rd, E2
Mon-Fri 11am–7pm;
Sun noon–6pm
Trendy as well as way-out fashions and accessories including red jeans, multicolored dresses and polka-dot spectacles.

Hoxton Boutique (C E1)
→ 2 Hoxton St, N1
Tue-Sat 11am–6.30pm (6pm Sat); Sun noon–5pm
A fabulous, mirror-lined store that was among the first to open in the area (2000) now selling its own avant-garde 'HOBO' fashion collection.

Brick Lane Market (C F1)
See the Welcome pages.

↑ Map I

WHITECHAPEL STREET
WHITE'S ROW
GUNTHORPE STREET
THRAWL STREET
FASHION ST
FOURNIER ST
PRINCELET STREET
HANBURY STREET
WOODSEER STREET
BUXTON STREET
WILKES STREET
GREY EAGLE STREET
QUAKER STREET
CALVIN STREET
HERAN STREET
CHILTON STREET
CHESHIRE STREET
SCLATER ST
WHITBY ST
BACON STREET
SWANFIELD STREET
CHAMBORD STREET
VIRGINIA ROAD
COLUMBIA ROAD
EZRA STREET
ALLEN GARDENS
OLD CASTLE ST
WENTWORTH ST
GOULSTON STREET
TOYNBEE STREET
BRUNE ST
BELL LANE
MIDDLESEX STREET
WHITES ROW
ARTILLERY LANE
CRISPIN STREET
GUN STREET
STEWARD STREET
BRUSHFIELD STREET
LAMB STREET
FOLGATE STREET
ELDER STREET
SPITAL STREET
CALVERT AVENUE
KINGSLAND RD
HACKNEY RD
BETHNAL GREEN ROAD
BRICK LANE
COMMERCIAL STREET
WENTWORTH STREET
HAMBURGH STREET
HARROW PLACE
GRAVEL LANE
MIDDLESEX STREET
CUTLER ST
DEVONSHIRE SQUARE
WORMWOOD STREET
HOUNDSDITCH
BISHOPSGATE
LIVERPOOL STREET
SUN STREET PASSAGE
APPOLD ST
PRIMROSE ST
EARL STREET
FINSBURY AVENUE
CHRISTOPHER STREET
WILSON STREET
SUN STREET
WORSHIP STREET
CLIFTON ST
HOLYWELL ROW
SCRUTTON STREET
HEWETT ST
PHIPP STREET
CURTAIN ROAD
LUKE ST
MARK ST
BLACKALL ST
WILLOW ST
NEW INN YARD
BATEMANS ROW
CHARLOTTE ROAD
RIVINGTON STREET
GREAT EASTERN STREET
SHOREDITCH HIGH ST
BOUNDARY ST
REDCHURCH ST
CLUB ROW
OLD NICHOL ST
CHANCE ST
NAVARRE ST
ARNOLD CIRCUS
PADBURY COURT
CLOSE
TOMLISON COURT
OLD ROAD
HOXTON STREET
CHART STREET
BOWLING GREEN WALK
BACHES STREET
BRUNSWICK PLACE
VINCE STREET
EAST RD
OLD STREET
COWPER STREET
LEONARD STREET
TABERNACLE STREET
EPWORTH STREET
PAUL STREET
BONHILL ST
DYSART ST
CITY ROAD
PLAYING FIELD
FINSBURY SQUARE
LACKINGTON ST
SOUTH PLACE
ELDON ST
MOORGATE PLACE
MOORGATE
BROADGATE
ST PAUL'S
LIVERPOOL STREET STATION
BISHOPSGATE INST
CHRIST CHURCH
OLD SPITALFIELDS MARKET
SPITAL SQUARE
BRICK LANE MARKET
WESLEY'S CHAPEL
CARPENTER'S HALL
LONDON WALL
COPTHALL AVENUE
FINSBURY CIRCUS
LIVERPOOL ST
BANK OF ...
ST MARGARET LOTHBURY
NAT. WESTMINSTER SAINT
SAINT ETHELBURGA
BALTIC
BISHOPSGATE CHURCHYARD
BEVIS MARKS
MAPLE ST
SPRAY ST
HOXTON
SPITALFIELDS
BETHNAL GREEN TECHNOLOGY COLL.

BANK OF ENGLAND MUSEUM

SS RE TOWER

MUSEUM OF LONDON

ST BARTHOLOMEW THE GREAT

SMITHFIELD MARKET

stained-glass windows.
Don't miss the art gallery,
which displays around
100 works illustrating
the history of London.

★ St Paul's Cathedral (C B3)

→ *St Paul's Churchyard, EC4
Mon-Sat 8.30am–4pm*
After the last war, the
cathedral was left standing
in the midst of the ruined
city. Churchill had protected
Wren's masterpiece, which
became the symbol of the
Londoners' indomitable
spirit in the face of the
enemy. Its dome, which took
35 years to reach
completion in 1708, is the
largest in the world after
that of St Peter's in Rome

and soars to a height of
361 ft. The Golden Gallery
at its summit offers
splendid views. The interior
boasts some splendid 18th-
century decorative
treasures: wrought-iron
choir gates by Tijou,
frescoes by Thornhill telling
the story of Saint Paul and
choir stalls by Gibbons. The
tombs of Wren and Nelson
are in the crypt.

★ Museum of London (C C2)

→ *London Wall, EC2
Tel. 0870 444 3850; Daily
10am (noon Sun)–5.50pm*
A fascinating museum
devoted to the story of
London and the life of its
people, from prehistory to

the present day. It offers
animated reconstructions
(including the Great Fire of
1666), models, everyday
items, relics and costumes.

★ St Bartholomew the Great (C B2)

→ *Church House, Cloth Fair,
EC1; Tue-Fri 8.30am–5pm;
Sat 10.30am– 4pm;
Sun 8.30am–8pm*
The oldest church in
London (12th century) has
had a checkered past. After
Henry VIII's ban on religious
orders in the 16th century,
the north transept was
used as a forge, the crypt
as a cellar, the Lady Chapel
as lodgings then as a
printing house, and the
cloister as a stable. The

church was restored and
again used for worship in
the 19th century. The
massive pillars of the
ambulatory are one of the
few examples of Norman
architecture in London.

★ Smithfield Market (C B2)

→ *Charterhouse St, EC1
Mon-Fri 3am–noon (come
before 7.30am)*
Monumental Victorian
buildings designed by
Sir Horace Jones in 1866–8
on a square which, in the
Middle Ages, used to stage
public executions. Since
1868 the beautiful cast-iron
arches, red-brick walls and
glass-roofed halls have
housed a meat market.

Map I →

LONDON CANAL MUSEUM

CAMDEN MARKETS

★ Charles Dickens Museum (D D4)
→ 48 Doughty St, WC1; Tel. 020 7405 2127; Daily 10am–5pm
The ticking of a clock is the only noise in this narrow, old-fashioned house where the great novelist Dickens (1812–70) lived from 1837 to 1839. Portraits and memorabilia, with a Victorian drawing room upstairs and, in the basement, a grille from the jail where his father was imprisoned for debt.

★ Foundling Museum (D D4)
→ 40 Brunswick Square, WC1 Tel. 020 7841 3600; Tue-Sat 10am–6pm; Sun noon–6pm
Opposite the garden where the Foundling Hospital (orphanage) stood until 1926 is a museum devoted to the life and work of Thomas Coram (1668–1751), who in 1739 opened the first institution for abandoned children in London. At street level in this elegant house, a poignant exhibition describes the misery of life in the streets contrasted with life in the refuge using engravings by Hogarth (1697–1764), objects, and photos. Upstairs is an exhibition of 18th-century works by philanthropic artists including canvases by Ramsay, Watson and Reynolds, and the stunning rococo Court Room.

★ Estorick Collection of Modern Italian Art (D E2)
→ 39 Canonbury Square, N1 Tel. 020 7704 9522; Tue-Sat 11am–6pm; Sun 1–5pm
This typical Georgian house displays the famous collection of modern Italian art belonging to Eric Estorick (1913–93). On view are key works by the pioneers of Futurism, a movement inspired by Cubism, speed and technology– Boccioni's Modern Idol (1911), Carrà's Leaving the Theater (1911), Severini's The Boulevard (1911), Russolo's Music (1911), and Balla's Rhythm of the Violinist (1912).

★ British Library (D C3)
→ 96 Euston Rd, NW1 Mon-Sat 9.30am–6pm (8, Tue; 5pm Sat); Sun 11am–
In 1997, after an overlor period of construction, new British Library fina opened its doors. The building's pure lines ar work of Colin St John W (1922–2007). With 14 fl totalling 190,000 squa of floor space, it contai collection begun in the century and considered be one of the greatest i world. Among the treas on view in the Sir John Ritblat Gallery, which c examined with the help tactile screens and list devices, are an illumin 15th-century Gutenber Bible, one of Leonardo

D

ESTORICK COLLECTION

FOUNDLING MUSEUM

CHARLES DICKENS MUSEUM

The north London that Dickens so vividly described is now no more than a memory: to the east, bars and boutiques line the sidewalks of Upper Street in Islington, now a smart part of town; while further south the superb new British Library (1997) and the new Eurostar Terminal (2007) at St Pancras Station have radically altered the old industrial area around King's Cross. Northwest of St Pancras lies the district of Camden Town, a mix of residential with attractive Victorian houses, and commercial, with the lively, touristy Camden market. To escape the crowds, especially at the weekend, follow the leafy canal to London Zoo, and go for a stroll in the nearby Regent's Park.

PASHA

NORTH SEA FISH

RESTAURANTS

Haché (D A2)
→ 24 Inverness St, NW1
Daily noon–10.30pm
A three-year-old family business whose venison, lamb, beef, fish and veggie burgers were voted 'best in London' by *TimeOut* readers last year. Very nice surroundings too. Burger £9.

Pasha (D E2)
→ 301 Upper St, N1
Daily 10am–11.30pm
Kebab with eggplant, ravioli filled with lamb, zucchini fritters and other Turkish delights in a smart, airy place with just the odd oriental flavor in the decor. Very friendly staff. Dishes, mezes £12.

North Sea Fish (D C4)
→ 7-8 Leigh St, WC1
Tel. 020 7387 5892; Mon-Sat noon–2.30pm, 6–10.30pm
Fresh fish includes Scottish salmon, undyed smoked haddock and homemade fishcakes, served with mushy peas – unadorned but tasty. Takeout fish and chips next door. Dishes £14.

Cottons (D A2)
→ 55 Chalk Farm Rd, NW1
Tel. 020 7485 8388; Mon-Fri 6–10.30pm; Sat noon–4pm, 6–11.30pm; Sun noon–10pm
A small restaurant and cocktail bar with a genuine Caribbean feel to it and terrific sweet-sour cuisine – coq au rhum, prawns with a papaya coulis, grills with plantain. Lively music too. Dishes £15.

Isarn (D E2)
→ 119 Upper St, N1
Tel. 020 7424 5153; Mon-Fri noon–3pm, 6–11pm; Sat noon–11pm (10.30pm Sun)
A modern Thai restaurant set up by Alan Yau's sister Tina and her Thai husband. Fresh, spicy, flavorsome cuisine is served in a thin, elegant black wood dining room. Try the steamed prawn and coconut dumpling, chargrilled swordfish with mint and lemongrass, and any of the curries, which are fantastic. Dishes £7–13.

Morgan M (D E2)
→ 489 Liverpool Rd, N7
Tel. 020 7609 3560; Wed-Fri, Sun from noon for lunch; Tue-Sat from 7pm for dinner
Those who arrive at this slightly out-of-the-way location are food lovers in the know, here for Morgan Meunier's successful French-rooted cuisine: pan-fried foie gras on toasted brioche with fig salad; roasted John Dory with carrot and ginger risotto. Three-course lunch £26; six-course dinner £48.

DUBLIN CASTLE

KOKO

BRITISH BOOT COMPANY

Moro (D E2)
→ 34-36 Exmouth Market, EC1; Tel. 0207 7833 8336
Mon-Sat 12.30–2.30pm; 7–10.30pm
Sam and Sam Clarke (husband and wife) are largely responsible for making the food of North Africa and Spain as fashionable as it is today in London. Moro is pricey, so sit at the long bar for tapas (served all day) rather than in the big dining room. Don't miss what may be the best bread in London, and the amazing range of sherries. Dishes £20. Tapas £3.50–4.

BAR, PUB

Angelic (D E3)
→ 57 Liverpool Rd, N1
Tel. 020 7278 8433; Daily noon–midnight (1am Fri-Sat)
A pub housed in the enormous old tavern that gave the adjacent subway station its name. Belgian beers, wines, milkshakes, tapas after 5pm and an extravagantly ornate lounge upstairs.

Dublin Castle (D A2)
→ 94 Parkway, NW1; Daily noon–1am (2am Fri-Sun)
This pub has become a local legend since bands from Madness to Amy

Winehouse have played on its tiny stage crammed into a corner of the bar. Pop, rock metal and indie every night from 8.30pm.

CLUB, CONCERT

KOKO (D B3)
→ 1a Camden High St, NW1
Fri-Sat 10pm–4am
This theater (1900) was beautifully restored and is now a landmark venue for rock and electro. Its purple rococo interior is the setting for seriously big concerts with dancing downstairs, by a mostly young, flamboyantly dressed, crowd.

The Round House (D A2)
→ Chalk Farm Rd, NW1
Tel. 087 0389 1846
www.roundhouse.org.uk
This refurbished locomotive shed (1846) was the setting for concerts by Jimi Hendrix, Pink Floyd and other immortals in the 1960s. Now it houses an eclectic mix of live music of all kinds as well as theater, dance, circus and cabaret.

SHOPPING

Lesley Craze Gallery (D E4)
→ 33-35a Clerkenwell Green, EC1; Tel. 020 7608 0393

Tue-Sat 10am–5.30pm
Contemporary fabrics and a wide selection of fantasy jewelry in a gallery-boutique dedicated to the work of young artists.

Exmouth Market (D E4)
A pedestrianized street lined with boutiques and cafés. At its best on Fridays and Saturdays when there is also a busy food market here.

Space EC1 (no. 25)
→ Mon-Fri 10.30am–6pm; Sat 11am–5pm
Printed pop-art paper, knitted hot-water-bottle covers, floral-patterned pots and pans, and other novelties.

Family Tree (no. 53)
→ Mon-Sat 11am–6pm
Rice paper lampshades decorated with motifs from traditional kimonos are among some of the unusual gifts and accessories on offer in this lifestyle store.

Camden Passage (D E3)
→ Wed and Sat (antiques & collectables); Thu (books) 10am–5pm
It's best to see this market on one of its antique days, with fantastic open-air displays of bygones. At other times there are bookstalls, jewelry kiosks and vintage clothes of the kind that

inspire young designers.

British Boot Company (D B2)
→ 5 Kentish Town Rd, NW1
Daily 10am–7pm
The legendary Dr Martens footwear, in production since 1958, has shod generations of skinheads, punks and rockers. This little store has a fantastic range of DMs as well as Grinders, George Cox and other iconic brand names.

Shikasuki (D A2)
→ 67 Gloucester Ave, NW1
Tel. 020 7722 4442
Daily 11am (noon Sun)–7pm
This smart clothes store just off Primrose Hill specializes in vintage models from 1930 to 1980 with evening gowns, jeweled coats and some fantastic geometric bags and other must-have accessories.

Upper Street (D E2)
You will find here an eclectic range of hip boutiques: After Noah (no. 121) for furniture, jewelry, gifts; Toast (no. 133) and Diverse (no. 294) for casual chic womenswear and accessories; Olivier Bonas (no. 147-8) for gifts, homeware, women's clothes; Igloo (no. 300) clothes, shoes, toys, etc. for children.

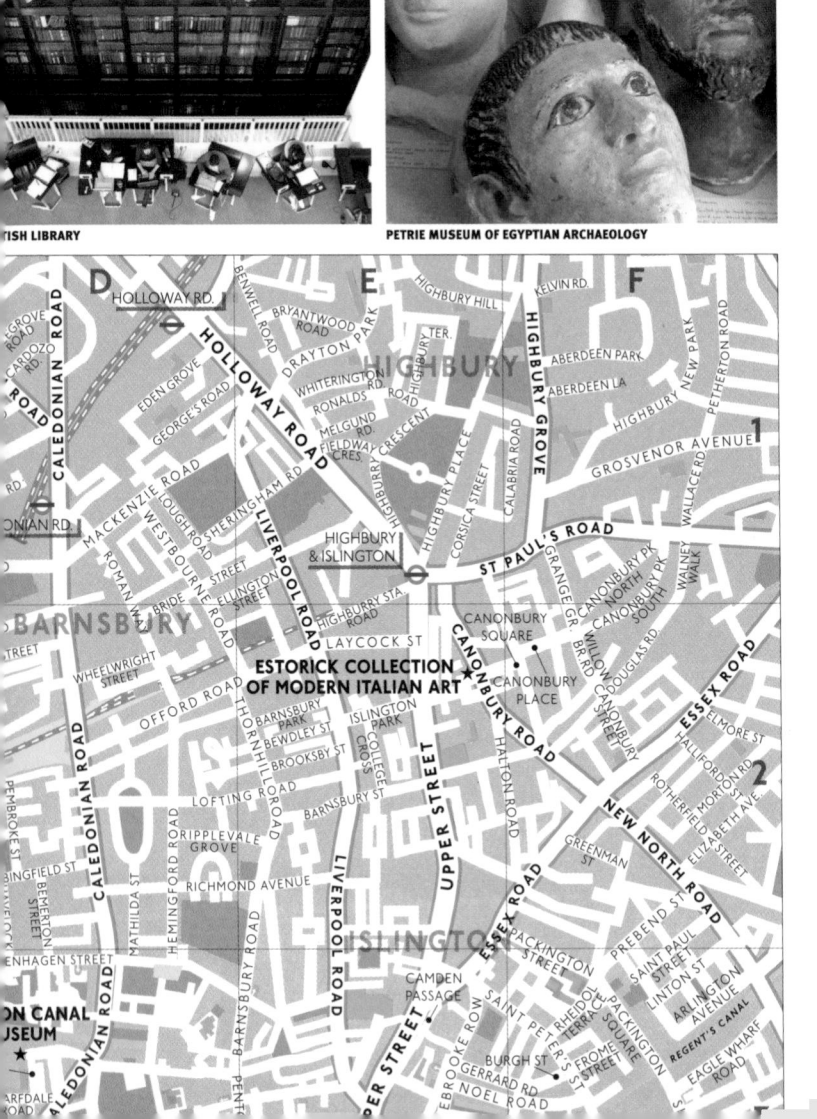

BRITISH LIBRARY

PETRIE MUSEUM OF EGYPTIAN ARCHAEOLOGY

ESTORICK COLLECTION OF MODERN ITALIAN ART

CAMDEN MARKETS

REGENT'S CANAL

LONDON ZOO

ci's notebooks,
nuscripts by Jane Austen,
rlotte Brontë, Lewis
oll, and the famous
na Carta, a charter of
onial rights signed by
g John in 1215 beside
Thames at Runnymede.

**Petrie Museum of
ptian Archaeology**
.4)
lalet Place, WC1
020 7679 2884; Tue–Fri
m; Sat 10am–1pm
display under the strip-
ing of a university
ding is the collection of
Egyptologist William
ers Petrie (1853–1942):
less objects such as
lry, statuettes, stelae,
horae, and a linen tunic

dating from 2800 BC.

★ **London
Canal Museum** (D D3)
→ 12-13 New Wharf Rd, N1
Tel. 020 7713 0836
Tue–Sun 10am–4.30pm
An ice-house built in 1862
by Carlo Gatti (1817–78),
an ice cream manufacturer,
has been converted into
a museum showing the
history of Britain's inland
waterways and the life of
the people who lived on
the narrow boats.

★ **Camden markets**
(D A2-B3)
→ Camden High St / Camden
Lock, NW1; Daily 10am–6pm
Less avant garde and edgy
than 15 years ago, parts of
Camden Market were

extensively modernized in
2007 and lost in character.
However Camden is still
lively and cosmopolitan, and
London's busiest market.
You'll find ready-to-wear,
jewelry, and vintage
accessories at Camden Lock;
furniture and antiques in the
new Stables Market, and
exotic fast food stalls
everywhere; on the store-
lined Camden High Street is
the open-air Buck Street
Market with around 200
clothes stalls. Go early to
avoid the teenage crowds.

★ **Regent's Canal** (D A2)
Opened in 1820, this 8-mile
canal links the docks to
Paddington, running along
the north side of Regent's

Park toward the leafy basin
of Little Venice. In good
weather the 3-miles walk
along the towpath from
Camden Lock with the
narrow boats and other
craft is a delight.

★ **London Zoo** (D A3)
→ Outer Circle, NW1; Daily
10am–5.30pm (4pm winter)
London's famous zoo
covers 36 acres. Since
opening in 1828, it has
ceaselessly sought to
improve the wellbeing
of its animals, housed
in 13 listed buildings.
More than 750 species
are represented, from
insects to giraffes,
including a splendid
collection of reptiles.

WALLACE COLLECTION

ALL SOULS CHURCH

The map shows part of Hyde Park and surrounding streets, including:
Sussex Square, Stanhope Terr, Hyde Park Gardens, Hyde Park Square, Park St, Albion St, Seymour, Marble Arch, Cumberland Gate, Bayswater Road, The Ring, North Ride, Speaker's Corner, Nursery, Ring Tea House, Hyde Park, Serpentine Road, The Serpentine, Rotten Row, South Carriage

0   100   200 m

★ **Regent's Park** (E C1)
→ *Daily 5am–sunset*
In 1811, John Nash, already a famous architect, obtained the backing of the future King George IV to realize his dream of creating an idealized garden city on farmland once belonging to the Duke of Portland. Nash wanted terraces around the sides of the park with high porticos, tall stuccoed façades and massive colonnades. Inside he envisaged grand mansions while more modest houses clustered together in romantic villages were to be situated around the perimeter. Only part of the dream was ever realized,

but this superb green space has many other attractions including tennis courts, cricket pitches, a zoo, the magnificent Queen Mary Rose Garden and the open-air theatre which stages *A Midsummer's Night's Dream* every summer.

★ **Madame Tussaud's Museum** (E C3)
→ *Marylebone Rd, NW1 Tel. 08709 990293; Daily 9.30am–5.30pm (6pm Sun)*
This famous waxworks is still the third most popular attraction in London. The Chamber of Horrors in the basement never fails to chill the heart. Next door is the former planetarium which now shows an animated

movie, *The Wonderful World of Stars*, by the same team who produced *Wallace and Gromit.*

★ **Sherlock Holmes Museum** (E B3)
→ *221b Baker St, NW1 Tel. 020 7935 8866 Daily 9.30am–6pm*
You are shown round the super-sleuth's Victorian apartments by his house-keeper, Mrs Hudson.

★ **Wallace Collection** (E C4)
→ *Manchester Square, W1 Tel. 020 7563 9551 Daily 10am–5pm*
The 4th Marquess of Hertford (1800–70) was a dandy, an eccentric and a well-informed collector. He

was passionately intere in painting (Hals, Frago Rembrandt, Velasquez, Poussin, Watteau), furn (Riesener and Boulle), objets d'art, and Easter and Western weaponry armor. His illegitimate h Richard Wallace, contin to swell this priceless collection which was bequeathed to the Stat 1897 on condition that works were never to lea the museum.

★ **Handel House Museum** (E D4)
→ *25 Brook St, W1; Tel. 0 7495 1685; Tue-Sat 10am (8pm Thu); Sun noon–6p concerts Thu 6.30pm*
Entered via a cobbled y

E

Map

ST JOHNS

NORFOLK SQUARE

ESSEX GARDENS

CAMBRIDGE SQUARE

EDG

GEORGE STREET

MONTAGU STREET

MONTAGU SQ.

MONTAGU SQ.

SEYMOUR

BRYANSTON SQ.

MEWS WEST

BRYANSTON ST

CLAY ST

GLOUCESTER PL

MARYLEBONE

NUTFORD PLACE

HARROWBY ST

BROWN ST

PRAED STREET

ST MICHAEL'S ST

STAR STREET

BRYANSTON PLACE

PADDINGTON BASIN

YORK

BICKENHALL ST

MAIN

ST MARY'S

CRAWFORD STREET

YORK STREET

HARCOURT

SHOULDHAM ST

TRANBPET STREET

CHAPEL ST

CHAPEL ST

EDGWARE ROAD

UPPER MONTAGU ST

KNOX ST

SAMARITAN HOSPITAL

NIGHTINGALE HOSPITAL

CHARTER

BELL STREET

NEWCASTLE PLACE

PENFOLD PLACE

3

RD.

BAN

CHAGFORD ST

GLOUCESTER PLACE

MARYLEBONE

MELCOMBE PLACE

DORSET SQUARE

MELCOMBE STREET

CHRIST CHURCH

COSWAY ST

LISSON STREET

SHROTON STREET

BROADLEY ST

EDGWARE ROAD

SHERLOCK HOLMES MUSEUM

★

LINHOPE ST

BALCOMBE ST

BOSTON PL

HAREWOOD AVE

MARYLEBONE STATION

HAREWOOD ROW

CHURCH STREET

ASHBRIDGE STREET

ASHMILL ST

PENFOLD STREET

LISSON GROVE

LISSON GROVE

ROSSMORE RD

CAPLAND ST

FRAMPTON STREET

SALISBURY STREET

LUTON ST

OUTER CIRCLE

BOATING LAKE

PARK ROAD

THRESHAM CRES

JEROME CRES

PAVELEY STREET

LODGE ROAD

NORTH BANK

2

SYNAGOGUE

WOOD ROAD

ST JOHNS WOOD ROAD

CENTRAL MOSQUE

LORD'S CRICKET GROUND

ST JOHN'S WOOD

PRINCE ALBERT ROAD

REGENT'S ROAD

WINFIELD HOUSE

OUTER CANAL

PRINCE ALBERT ROAD

CIRCLE

B

ST JOHN'S TERRACE

ST JOHN'S WOOD TERRACE

CHARLES LANE

EAMONT ST

CHARLBERT STREET

ALLITSEN ROAD

BRIDGEMAN ST

NEW COURT

ST JOHN'S WOOD HIGH ST

NEWCOURT ST

CAVENDISH AVE

WELLINGTON ROAD

WELLINGTON PL

COCHRANE ST

1

A

MADAME TUSSAUD'S MUSEUM

REGENT'S PARK

Mayfair has the reputation of being the classiest district in London. Although Vivienne Westwood, the subversive creator of the 1970s' punk look, opened a shop here, the prestigious hotels and luxury stores on New and Old Bond streets are more in keeping with the district's upmarket image. Marylebone, further north, is more lively, particularly around Marylebone High Street, with its striking Georgian façades and astonishing array of clothes shops and good restaurants. Around Regent's Park there are many neoclassical marvels including John Nash's magnificent Cumberland Terrace, with its blue and white pediment in the east.

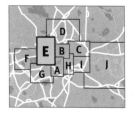

SEASHELL

FISHWORKS

RESTAURANTS

Seashell (E A3)
→ 49-51 Lisson Grove, NW1
Tel. 020 7224 9000; Mon-Fri
noon–2.30pm, 5–10.30pm;
Sat noon–10.30pm
Excellent fish & chips with a light, airy green setting and big marble counters. Dishes £11.

Carluccio's Caffè (E C4)
→ St Christopher's Place, W1
Mon-Fri 8am–11pm;
Sat-Sun 9am–10.30pm
One of the many deli-restaurants of Italian chef Antonio Carluccio. Eat in or take out. Dishes £12. If Italian doesn't appeal don't worry: this is only one of the dozens eateries lining St Christopher's Place and James Street.

Ping Pong (F C3)
→ 29a James St, W1; also
10 Paddington St (F C2)
Daily noon–11pm
A good spot for affordable, high-quality dim sum and fragrant steamed dumplings – try the king prawns and bamboo shoots or snow crab, prawns and scallops in carrot tortellini pastry. Black, soothing decor and friendly staff. From £3 per portion (plan at least four per person). Interesting cocktails (try the vodka with lemongrass, lime and lychee or kumquat mojito).

Rocket (E D5)
→ 4-6 Lancashire Court, W1
Tel. 020 7629 2889; Mon-Sat
noon–3pm, 6–11pm
There's no pasta in this cozy pizzeria, furnished with velvet armchairs, but a choice of enormous and imaginative salads and melt-in-the-mouth pizzas with any topping you choose – hence the queue. Pizza £13.

Maroush III (E B4)
→ 62 Seymour St, W1
Daily noon–midnight
A well-established empire of Lebanese restaurants – named Maroush, Ranoush and Sidi Maarouf – priding itself on offering good food and good service. The traditional mezes, wraps, shawarmas, chargrilled meats, etc. are faultless. Meze £5; dishes £13.

**The Providores
and Tapa Room** (E C3)
→ 109 Marylebone High St,
W1; Tel. 020 7935 6175
Mon-Fri 9am–11pm;
Sat-Sun 10am–10.30pm
The relaxed Tapa Room at street level is a smart combination of breakfast-, tapas-, and wine-bar. Excellent all-day menu, a fusion of Eastern and Western flavors: edamame and feta tortilla with Greek yoghurt and rocket, fried

MORE HALL

OLD BOND STREET

CHARBONNEL & WALKER

manouri cheese with a black fig and pomegranate dressing. Tapa £4–9. The restaurant is upstairs (dishes £11–25).

Nagomi (E D4)
→ 4 Blenheim St, W1
Tel. 020 7165 9506; Mon-Sat noon–3pm, 6–11pm
Movable panels separate the kitchen from the dining room in this intriguing Japanese interior. Delicacies include octopus fritters, chicken stuffed with prawns, and a delicious rice cake with beans. Sushi £3–4, selection £13.

Fishworks (E C3)
→ 89 Marylebone High St, W1; Tel. 020 7935 9796
Mon-Fri, Sun noon–3pm, 6–10.30pm; Sat noon–10.30pm
Award-winning branch of a 12-outlet chain, set behind the fishmonger's shop-front. Small, informal room and sensational sea produce. Reservation advised. Dishes £20.

TEAROOMS

The Conservatory (E C6)
→ Lanesborough Hotel, Hyde Park Corner, SW1
Tel. 020 7259 5599
Daily 3.30–6pm (4pm Sun)
Be more British than the British and sample the delights of afternoon tea

in one of London's most stylish hotels, across from Hyde Park. Delicate sandwiches and scones with jams and clotted cream are served in a tiered winter garden.

De Gustibus (E C4)
→ 53 Blandford St, W1
Tel. 020 7486 6608
Mon-Fri 6.30am–4pm
Artisan bakers are getting rare, so it is a genuine pleasure to sit in this traditional bakery lined with wrought-iron shelves and pots of jam. Fantastic breads and patisseries, obviously.

The Parlour at Sketch (E D4)
→ 9 Conduit St, W1
Mon-Sat 8am (10am Sat)–2am; Tea: Mon-Sat 3–7.30pm
The Parlour occupies the ground floor of the flamboyant Sketch complex. Tables and chairs that don't match and a chandelier made of Anglepoise lamps are just two of the quirky touches in this eccentric spot. The restrooms too are worth a visit.

CONCERTS

Wigmore Hall (E D4)
→ 36 Wigmore St. W1
Tel. 020 7935 2141
www.wigmore-hall.org.uk

Built in 1901 by the Bechstein Piano firm, this building is a gem of a recital hall with fantastic acoustics. Chamber music and songs.

SHOPPING

Geo F. Trumper (E D5)
→ 9 Curzon St, W1
Tel. 020 7499 1850; Mon-Fri 9am–5.30pm; Sat 9am–1pm
Shaving brushes in all shapes and sizes, razors, colognes and aftershaves: the last word in men's beauty products. Drop in for a perfect shave, manicure (except Sat) or haircut at one of the most famous gentleman's stores in the city.

Selfridges (E C4)
→ 400 Oxford St, W1
Mon-Sat 9.30am–8pm (9pm Thu); Sun noon–6pm
Huge department store stocking most fashion labels, with something to suit everyone's purse. Well known for its menswear collections, postcard shop and food hall (although the latter doesn't compare with Harrods').

Topshop Topman (E D4)
→ 214 Oxford St, W1
Mon-Sat 9am–9pm; Sun noon–6pm
A temple to fashion, with all the latest styles at

affordable prices: coats, dresses, tee-shirts, jeans, jewelry, shoes, and more for ladies and gents of all ages – babies included.

Old and New Bond streets (E D4-5)
The epitome of elegant shopping. Among the many shops are: **Smythson of Bond Street** for leatherbound stationery. **Alexander McQueen, MaxMara, Bulgari, Prada, Armani** for men's and women's fashion. **DeBeers, Tiffany, Bentley & Skinner, Asprey** for some of the most beautiful jewelry in the world. And **Charbonnel & Walker**, the queen's favorite chocolates, flavored with lavender, raspberry, mint, rose or violet, made in the time-honored English tradition.

Alfie's Antique Market (E A3)
→ 13-15 Church St, NW8
Tel. 020 7723 6066
Tue-Sat 10am–6pm
Opened in 1976 on the site of an old department store, this covered market has gradually grown to become the largest in the country with five floors of antiques from all over the world, including lots of 20th-century design artefacts from the 1920s up to the age of pop art.

ZOOLOGICAL GARDENS

BROAD WALK

ST JOHN

ALBANY STREET

OUTER CIRCLE

MORNINGTON TER

PARK EAST VILLAGE

ENT'S PARK

OUTER CIRCLE

★

REGENT'S PARK

AUGUSTUS STREET

Cumberland Market

STANHOPE STREET

INNER CIRCLE

BROAD WALK

ALBANY STREET

OUTER CIRCLE

ROBERT STREET

Clarence Gardens

"EEN MARY'S GARDENS

★

Munster Square

LAXTON SQUARE

2

EGENT'S COLLEGE

OSNABURGH STREET

PARK SQ. EAST

HOLY TRINITY

GREAT PORTLAND ST

EUSTON ROAD

MADAME TUSSAUD'S MUSEUM

OUTER CIRCLE

YORK TERRACE EAST

PARK SQUARE GARDENS

PARK SQ. WEST

REGENT'S PARK

PARK CRESCENT MEWS WEST

PARK CRESCENT

CLEVELAND ST

DON MARYLEBONE RD.

ST MARYLEBONE

ROYAL ACADEMY OF MUSIC

ROYAL NAT. ORTH. HOSPITAL

KARIUM

OLDBURY ST

DEVONSHIRE PLACE

DEVONSHIRE MEWS WEST

DEVONSHIRE STREET

CARBURTON STREET

LUXBOROUGH STREET

MARYLEBONE HIGH ST

HARLEY STREET

PORTLAND PLACE

GREAT PORTLAND STREET

BOLSOVER STREET

GREAT TITCHFIELD ST

3

PADDINGTON ST

DEVONSHIRE HOSPITAL

WEYMOUTH STREET

HALLAM STREET

MOXON STREET

AYBROOK STREET

MARYLEBONE STREET

WEYMOUTH MEWS

NEW CAVENDISH ST

MANSFIELD STREET

ST CHILTERN STREET

FENWICK

BLANDFORD ST

WELBECK STREET

WIMPOLE STREET

HARLEY PLACE

QUEEN ANNE ST

LANGHAM STREET

Langham Place BBC

MORTIMER ST

LITTLE PORTLAND ST

RD KENDALL PLACE

JARE BAKER ST

GEORGE ST

★ **WALLACE COLLECTION**

R. ADAM STREET

WIGMORE HALL

ALL SOULS CHURCH

★

MANCHESTER SQUARE

MARYLEBONE LA

WIGMORE ST

CAVENDISH ST

WIMPOLE STREET

UNIVERSITY OF WESTMINSTER

REGENT

TMAN JARE DENS

WIGMORE ST

CHRIST

JOHN LEWIS

OXFORD CIRCUS

4

ON

HANDEL HOUSE MUSEUM

SHEPHERD MARKET

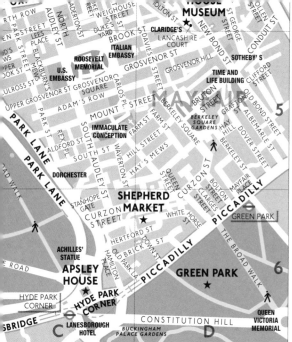

APSLEY HOUSE

HYDE PARK

house where Handel ⬦5–1759) lived from 1723 l his death, and where omposed *Messiah*, been carefully recreated how his living quarters music room with es, paintings and a fine y of an 18th-century sichord.

hepherd ⬦ket (E D6)
⬦etween Curzon St and ⬦dilly
t of crowded Piccadilly, haven of peace calls ind a little hamlet aded with pedestrian ts and scattered with ealing paved tyards. This used to be ⬦enter of the May Fairs

(cereals and cattle) from which the entire area derived its name.

★ **All Souls Church (E** D4)
→ *Langham Place, W1
Mon-Fri 10am–6pm;
Sun 9.30am–6.30pm*
When it was completed in 1824, this church, the only one built by John Nash that is still standing, was likened by some critics to a wedding cake.

★ **Apsley House (E** C6)
→ *Hyde Park Corner, W1
Tel. 020 7499 5676; Tue-Sun
10am–5pm (4pm Oct-March)*
'Number One, London', as the house is also known, was given to Wellington as a reward for his victory over Napoleon at the Battle

of Waterloo (1815). He was also given many paintings and precious objects by influential figures, a collection which he enhanced with various spoils of war. Paintings by great masters (Velasquez, Goya, Rubens, etc.); sculpture (Canova's Naked Napoleon); silver and gold plate; and priceless porcelain. Unfortunately the museum does not have a pair of the Iron Duke's famous Wellington boots.

★ **Hyde Park (E** B6)
→ *Daily 5am–midnight*
London's most popular park is like an immense green lung at the city's center. Bathers, boats and swans

play up and down the Serpentine, where a midnight swim is held every year at Christmas. Riders parade along Rotten Row and the lawns are inviting for a siesta. Since 1872, would-be orators have aired their opinions at Speaker's Corner; anyone can stand on a makeshift platform and have their say here as they attempt to rally passersby to their cause.

★ **Green Park (E** D6)
Extensive lawns, shady plane and lime trees, cast-iron benches and old gas lamps. Originally a leper's burial ground, no flowers are planted as a mark of respect for the dead below.

HOLLAND PARK

HOLLAND PARK

NOTTING HILL

★ Serpentine Gallery (F F3)
→ *Kensington Gardens W2*
Tel. 020 7402 6075
Daily 10am–6pm
A pretty tea pavilion (1934) surrounded by greenery, which was turned into an art gallery in 1970 and stages exhibitions of, and special events relating to, modern and contemporary art. Man Ray, Henry Moore, Andy Warhol, Bridget Riley, Damien Hirst and Rachel Whiteread are just a few of the artists who have exhibited here.

★ Kensington Gardens (F E2-3)
→ *Daily 6am–sunset*
Originally a playground for the nation's young queens, it is now a children's paradise with model boats sailing on the Round Pond, a statue of Peter Pan, puppet shows in the summer and two play areas. The flower beds and water features in the Sunken Gardens, hidden by the foliage of lime trees, are reminiscent of Tudor gardens.

★ Kensington Palace (F D3)
→ *Kensington Palace Gardens W8*
Tel. 087 0751 5176; Daily 10am–6pm (5pm Nov-Feb)
In 1689, King William III, afflicted with asthma, decided to take advantage of Kensington's pure air. He asked Christopher Wren and Nicholas Hawksmoor to enlarge the existing brick and white stone manor house and turn it into a royal residence. Between 1689 and 1837 all the British rulers lived and died here. Princess Victoria was baptized in the Cupola Room in 1819 and held her first privy council in the Red Saloon on the day she ascended the throne. The apartments are resplendent with oak paneling, trompe-l'œil designs on the ceilings and walls, portraits of members of the royal family and the furniture which once belonged to them.

★ Linley Sambourne House (F C4)
→ *18 Stafford Terrace, W8*
Tel. 020 7602 3316
Guided tours mid-March–
Oct: Sat-Sun 11.15am, 1pm,
2.15pm, 3.30pm
A miraculously preserved Victorian interior, where the *Punch* cartoonist Edward Linley Sambourne lived from 1874 to 1910, was also a disciple of the Aesthetic Movement that sought to find purity of form by imitating natural lines and shapes. There are many examples of his caricatures on the walls and most of the interior decoration, including the

F

SERPENTINE GALLERY

KENSINGTON GARDENS

A · B · C

BASSETT RD

GOLBORNE ROAD

OXFORD GDNS.

OXFORD GARDENS

CAMBRIDGE GDNS.

CAMBRIDGE GDNS.

LADBROKE GROVE

ACKLAM ROAD

WESTWAY

WESTWAY

LANCASTER ROAD

TAVISTOCK ROAD

BASING STREET

PORTOBELLO ROAD

LUKE'S RD

ALL SAINTS ROAD

ST LUKE'S RD

LEAMINGTON ROAD VILLAS

POWIS MEWS

POWIS GDNS.

POWIS TERRACE

LEBURY ROAD

LEBURY ROAD

SHREWSBURY ROAD

TALBOT ROAD

NORTHUMBERLAND PLACE

MOORHOUSE ROAD

SUTHERLAND PLACE

COURTNELL STREET

ARTESIAN RD

LEDBURY ROAD

SAINT STEPHENS GDNS.

CHEPSTOW ROAD

TALBOT ROAD

KILDARE TERRACE

HEREFORD ROAD

BRIDSTOW PL.

TALBOT ROAD

WEST

HEREFORD ROAD

CHEPSTOW PLACE

LADBROKE GROVE

MARK'S RD

WESTWAY

LANCASTER RD

CAMELFORD WALK

MARK'S ROAD

CORNWALL CRESCENT

BLENHEIM CRESCENT

BLENHEIM CRESCENT

LADBROKE GROVE

KENSINGTON PARK ROAD

ELGIN CRESCENT

ELGIN CRES.

PORTOBELLO ROAD

PORTOBELLO ROAD

COLVILLE SQUARE

COLVILLE TERR.

COLVILLE ROAD

TALBOT ROAD

LONSDALE ROAD

SO

POWIS SQUARE

WESTBOURNE PARK ROAD

WESTBOURNE GROVE

PEMBRIDGE VILLAS

PEMBRIDGE VILLAS

PEMBRIDGE RD

CHEPSTOW VILLAS

CHEPSTOW ROAD

DAWSON PLACE

PEMBRIDGE PLACE

PEMBRIDGE SQUARE

BAYSW

LINDEN GDNS.

ARUNDEL GARDENS

LADBROKE GARDENS

ROSMEAD ROAD

LANSDOWNE ROAD

STANLEY CRES.

DENBIGH ROAD

DENBIGH CRES.

PEMBRIDGE CRES.

PORTOBELLO ROAD

PORTOBELLO ROAD MARKET ★

NOTTING HILL ★

CLARENDON ROAD

WALMER ROAD

MARY PL.

SIRDAR RD

WILSHAM STREET

LANSDOWNE CRESCENT

PORTLAND ROAD

KENSINGTON PARK GARDENS

LADBROKE SQUARE GARDENS

ST JOHN'S GDNS.

LANSDOWNE WALK

CLARENDON ROAD

LANSDOWNE RD

KENSINGTON PARK RD

LADBROKE GROVE

LADBROKE SQUARE

LADBROKE TER.

KENSINGTON PARK ROAD

PEMBRIDGE GARDENS

PEMBRIDGE GDNS.

NOTTING HILL GATE

NOTTING HILL GATE

HILL GA

PALACE

NOTTING

HILLGATE STREET

KENSINGTON PLACE

ST JAME'S GARDENS

ST JAME'S GARDENS

PRINCEDALE ROAD

LADBROKE ROAD

HILLSLEIGH RD

CAMPDEN HILL

CAMPDEN HILL SQUARE

AUBREY ROAD

AUBREY WALK

CAMPDEN HILL ROAD

PEEL STREET

CAMPDEN STREET

KENSINGTON PLACE

BEDFORD GARDENS

SHEFFIELD TERRACE

KENSINGTON CHU

BRUNSWI

ST ANN'S VILLA

ROYAL CRES.

QUEENSDALE ROAD

ADDISON AVENUE

NORLAND SQUARE

HOLLAND PARK

HOLLAND PARK AVENUE

HOLLAND PARK MEWS

HOLLAND PARK

HOLLAND WALK

PK. GDN.

CESTER CHU

Kensington, a holiday resort on the outskirts of the city even before Kensington Palace became the royal residence in 1689, still has a split personality. It is both a busy shopping center, with its many stores on Kensington High Street, and a prestigious residential area made up of stately houses and converted mews buildings. The influx of wealthy professionals and celebrities to the north of Notting Hill Gate has overturned its former reputation as a ghetto. A sensational carnival is organized at the end of every August by the African and West-Indian community living around Portobello Road.

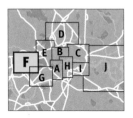

TAQUERIA

LAZY DAISY CAFÉ

RESTAURANTS

Taqueria (F C2)
→ 139 Westbourne Grove, W11; Daily noon–11pm
This small Mexican diner has an extensive menu of sopas, tostadas, tacos with extra fresh ingredients and homemade, soft corn tortillas. Try one of the aguas frescas with lime, guava, cucumber or a margarita. Dishes £5.50.

Costa's (F C2)
→ 18 Hillgate St, W8; Tue-Sat noon–2.30pm, 6–10.30pm
Generous portions of fresh fish & chips, squid, scampi, fishcakes and the like. Eat in or take out. Dishes £7.

The Cow (F C1)
→ 89 Westbourne Park Rd, W2; Tel. 020 7221 0021; Mon-Sat noon–4pm, 6–11pm; Sun 12.30–3.30pm, 7–10pm
A trendy Notting Hill hangout, it is a friendly Irish bar downstairs, serving fresh oysters and Guinness, and a relaxed gastropub upstairs, with an accent on seafood. Dishes £13 (upstairs).

Maggie Jones (F D3)
→ 6 Old Court Place W8 Tel. 020 7937 6462; Daily 12.30–2.30pm, 6.30–11pm
This three-story, quirky restaurant off the busy High Street looks like an old farmhouse, with wooden floorboards, snug nooks and crannies, and wine bottles serving as candle holders. Simple British fare of a high standard: steak and kidney pie, saddle of lamb, bread and butter pudding. Dishes £18.50. Set Sun lunch £18.

The Belvedere (H B4)
→ Holland Park, next to the car park off Abbotsbury Rd, W8; Tel. 020 7602 1238 Daily noon–2.30pm, 6–11pm; closed Sun dinner
An oasis of elegance and tranquillity in the heart of Holland Park, with parquet floors, high-ceilinged windows and small round tables looking out onto greenery. There's also a magnificent terrace to eat al fresco in summer – with few tables so reserve. Delicious, unpretentious, modern British cuisine. Pre- or post-theater menu £22.

TEAROOMS

The Orangery (F D3)
→ Kensington Palace, W8 Tel. 020 7376 0239 Daily 10am–6pm
What better setting for traditional high tea (scones, jams, and sandwiches) than this large, light, and airy greenhouse designed

BROKE ARMS

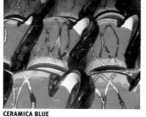

CERAMICA BLUE

RELLIK

by Sir John Vanbrugh for Queen Anne in 1704.

Lazy Daisy Café (F C2)
→ *59a Portobello Rd, W11*
Mon-Sat 9am–5pm;
Sun noon–2.30pm
Need a cozy break to escape the market's weekend crowds? Salads, soups, baked potatoes, teas, and homemade cakes. Eat on the paved courtyard if the sun is out.

BARS, PUBS, CLUB, MOVIES

Churchill Arms (F C3)
→ *119 Kensington Church St,*
W8; Tel. 020 7727 4242
Mon-Sat 11am–11pm
(midnight Thu-Sat); Sun
noon–10.30pm
The walls and ceilings of this large pub are hung with countless objects: wicker baskets, copper utensils, butterflies, paintings, photographs. Very popular both for its atmosphere and for the excellent and cheap Thai food – so you may find it hard to get a table.

Julie's Wine Bar (F A2)
→ *135 Portland Rd, W11*
Tel. 020 7727 7985; Daily
9am–11.30pm (10pm Sun)
A haven of calm a few minutes walk from Portobello Road market and a romantic place for

drink. Sit on the shady terrace or step inside where, over two floors, alcoves form Andalusian-style lounges with plants and some fine oriental touches to the decor.

Ladbroke Arms (F B2)
→ *54 Ladbroke Rd, W11*
Daily noon–11pm
(10.30pm Sun)
A welcoming pub in a little yellow house, with open fires, comfy maroon seats and a terrace. It also serves very good pub food.

**Nottinghillartsclub
(F** C2)
→ *1 Notting Hill Gate, W11*
Mon-Fri 6pm–2am; Sat-Sun
4pm–2am (1am Sun)
A basement club with two dance floors, featuring a lot of alternative world music: Latino funk, Asian drum 'n' bass, Gypsy punk, and other wild sounds.

Electric Cinema (F B2)
→ *191 Portobello Rd, W11*
Tel. 020 7908 9696
A mythical movie theater (and the first in London, dating from 1911). Coming to see a movie here is a special experience – comfortable leather seating or two-seater sofas with footstools, and side tables for snacks from the bar. Mainstream and art house programs.

The Electric Brasserie next door is open for breakfast, lunch, and dinner.

SHOPPING

Paul Smith (F B1)
→ *Westbourne Grove,*
122 Kensington Park Rd, W11
Mon-Sat 10am–6pm
(6.30pm Sat)
Magnificent shop with collections for men, women and children by one of the stars of English fashion. Materials with exquisite patterns and colors are combined with classic cuts and retro or ethnic touches.

Urban Outfitters (F C4)
→ *36-38 Kensington High*
St, W8; Mon-Sat 10am–7pm
(8pm Thu); Sun 11am–6pm;
other branches in London
This immense concrete space is filled with an organized chaos of fashionable clothes, household objects, cards, world music cds, and accessories.

**Blenheim
Crescent (F** A1)
The Spice Shop (no. 1)
→ *Mon-Sat 9.30am–6pm;*
Sun 11am–4pm
The brightly colored shop front conceals an Ali-Baba's cave of treasures: dried fruit, aromatic herbs and spices, etc.

Books for Cooks (no. 4)
→ *Mon-Sat 10am–6pm*
Cook books from floor to ceiling and a tiny kitchen with a few tables at he back, which tries out recipes from some of the volumes on sale for lunch (arrive early).

Ceramica Blue (no. 10)
→ *Mon-Sat 10am–6.30pm;*
Sun noon–5pm
The tableware, tiles and giftware on offer here are the work of 20 potters from different countries. Super colors and craftsmanship.

202 (F B1)
→ *202 Westbourne Grove*
W11; Mon-Sat 8.30am (10am
Mon)–6pm; Sun 10am–5pm
A concept store by Nicole Farhi, part fashionable café, part fashion store. It stocks women's and children's clothes, objets d'art and accessories the designer found while traveling around the world.

Rellik (F A1)
→ *8 Golborne Rd, W10*
Tel. 020 8962 0089
Tue-Sat 10am–6pm
At the foot of the huge 30-story Trellik Tower is one of the best vintage clothes stores in London, opened by three former dealers from Portobello Road with models by Vivienne Westwood, Terri Havilland, Bill Gibb and others.

SERPENTINE GALLERY

RING

LANCASTER W

THE

PALACE

PA

ROUND POND

KENSINGTON PALACE

PALACE GARDENS

THE ORANGERY

PHYSICAL ENERGY STATUE

KENSINGTON GARDENS

THE BROAD WALK

BUDGE'S WALK

LANCASTER WALK

THE RING

THE LONG WATER

BUDGE'S WALK

NORTH WALK

2

NORTH WALK

BAYSWATER ROAD

QUEENSWAY

LANCASTER GATE

LANCASTER GATE NEWS

BAYSWATER ROAD

HILL GDNS

LANCASTER TERR.

STANHOPE TERRACE

Sussex Square

GRAVEN TER.

CRAVEN HILL

PORCHESTER TERRACE

INVERNESS TERRACE

WAY

BARK PLACE

ST PETERSBURGH PLACE

ST JAMES'S

GRAVEN GDNS

QUEENSBOROUGH TERRACE

QUEENS

GLOUCESTER TERRACE

ROAD

SUSSEX GARDENS

SUSSEX GARDENS

SPRING ST

CHILWORTH STREET

DEVONSHIRE TERRACE

QUEENS GARDENS

LEINSTER GARDENS

CLEVELAND SQUARE

CLEVELAND GARDENS

PORCHESTER TERRACE

PORCHESTER GDNS

QUEENSWAY

REDAN PL.

SALEM ROAD

KENSINGTON SQ.

PADDINGTON

GLOUCESTER TERRACE

1

STAR STREET

PRAED STREET

NORFOLK SQUARE

LONDON STREET

BISHOP'S BRIDGE ROAD

INVERNESS TERRACE

QUEENSWAY

GROVE

PAUL'S

PADDINGTON STATION

SOUTH WHARF ROAD

EASTBOURNE TERRACE

TER

ORSETT TER.

GLOUCESTER TER.

TERRACE NORTH

PORCHESTER

QUEENSWAY

WESTBOURNE GARDENS

TER

WESTBOURNE TERRACE

WESTBOURNE BRIDGE ROAD

WESTBOURNE TERRACE

BRIDGE RD

ROAD

GLOUCESTER

OYAL OAK

SINGTON PALACE

F

E

D

LEIGHTON HOUSE

LINLEY SAMBOURNE HOUSE

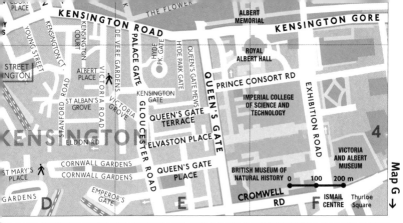

KENSINGTON ROAD

THE FLOWER

ALBERT MEMORIAL

KENSINGTON GORE

YOUNG STREET

KENSINGTON COURT

KENSINGTON CT.

DE VERE GARDENS

PALACE GATE

HYDE PK. GATE

HYDE PARK GATE

QUEEN'S GATE MEWS

ROYAL ALBERT HALL

STREET NGTON

ALBERT PLACE

VICTORIA GROVE

ST ALBAN'S GROVE

ST. ALBAN'S GROVE

KENSINGTON GATE

PRINCE CONSORT RD

IMPERIAL COLLEGE OF SCIENCE AND TECHNOLOGY

EXHIBITION ROAD

KENSINGTON

STANFORD ROAD

VICTORIA ROAD

ELDON RD

QUEEN'S GATE TERRACE

GLOUCESTER ROAD

ELVASTON PLACE

QUEEN'S GATE

EXHIBITION ROAD

VICTORIA AND ALBERT MUSEUM

4

ST MARY'S PLACE

CORNWALL GARDENS

CORNWALL GARDENS

QUEEN'S GATE PLACE

BRITISH MUSEUM OF NATURAL HISTORY

0   100   200 m

GARDENS

EMPEROR'S GATE

CROMWELL RD

ISMAIL CENTRE

Thurloe Square

D   E   F

Map G →

ING HILL

PORTOBELLO ROAD MARKET

papers, is the work of am Morris.

eighton House (F B4)
 Holland Park Rd, W14
 20 7602 3316
 Mon 11am–5.30pm
vagance reigns
eme behind the
sical façade. Frederick
Leighton, artist and
dent of the Royal
emy, was a keen
ler and orientalist.
anted red walls in
tyle of a Venetian
ce, and an Arab hall
hy of an Eastern
ce. The house had
ything, including
ce tiles from Iznik and
entle murmur of a
ain. Also on display is

a wonderful collection of pre-Raphaelite paintings by Leighton's friends, particularly canvases by Burne-Jones and Millais.
★ **Holland Park (F** B3)
→ Daily 8am–9pm
The most romantic and densely wooded of London's parks comprises a group of small gardens (the Dutch, Rose, Iris and Japanese gardens) which are home to strutting peacocks. All that remains of Holland House (1605), the Dutch-style manor house to which these lands once belonged, is the west wing, a rare vestige of the Jacobean period. On summer evenings plays,

ballets and operas are performed on the terrace. The park also has a gourmet restaurant (see previous page) and a café.
★ **Notting Hill (F** B2)
At night the pubs in Westbourne Park Road act as a magnet for the young and trendy, the stars and starlets, and of couse the locals. Notting Hill, a somewhat neglected district until the 1990s, became popular with young wealthy professionals hungry for a more diverse, Bohemian atmosphere. Georgian houses stand on the higher ground, streets on the slopes are lined with pastel houses and more

dilapidated districts extend further north. Over the last weekend in August a million people throng the streets for a spectacular fancy-dress parade and festival, organized by the area's West Indian residents since the 1960s.
★ **Portobello Road Market (F** B2-A1)
→ Portobello Rd / Golborne Rd, W11; Mon-Sat 8am–7pm (1pm Thu)
This huge market is a must on Saturdays when fruit and vegetable stalls jostle for space with stalls selling antiques, second-hand clothes and bric-a-brac.

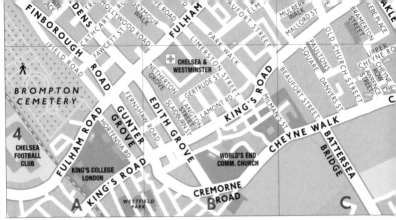

BELGRAVE SQUARE

SAATCHI GALLERY

★ Christie's South Kensington (G B2)

→ 85 Old Brompton Rd, SW7
Tel. 020 7930 6074
Mon-Fri 9am–5pm (7.30pm Mon); Sat-Sun 10am–4pm
Visit the illustrious dealer where objets d'art and other items are auctioned.

★ Natural History Museum (G B2)

→ Cromwell Rd, SW7; Tel. 020 7942 5000; Daily 10am–5.50pm; www.nhm.ac.uk
Even the façade of the museum, one of Europe's largest, is swarming with plants and animals. There are 78 million specimens kept here, but only a small part of the collection is exhibited, charting the history and diversity of life on Earth, from dinosaurs to earthquakes. This is a fascinating museum but so big it is a good idea to plan your visit with the help of the website or a guide at the museum.

★ Science Museum (G C1)

→ Exhibition Rd, SW7; Tel. 020 7942 4000; Daily 10am–6pm
A museum at the cutting edge of scientific progress. Interactive attractions and simulations abound on the four floors, an amazing showcase for the latest in scientific development (cloning, the most recent mission to Mars, advances in genetic engineering). The old rooms focus on the leading inventions of the industrial era, including a V2 missile, the Apollo 10 command module or George Stephenson's *Rocket*.

★ Victoria & Albert Museum (G C2)

→ Cromwell Rd, SW7
Tel. 020 7942 2000; Daily 10am–5.45pm (10pm Fri)
The 'V&A' houses one of the world's great collections of decorative arts. Exhibition galleries stretch for over 6 miles, and 4 million pieces are on display in 146 rooms. There is a vast variety of European and Asiatic objects including Raphael's tapestry cartoons, Indian fabrics and Korean ceramics. The section o[f] Indian art is unmatched[ed] outside India. Fifteen B[ritish] Galleries tell the story o[f] British design from the reign of Henry VIII to th[e] Queen Victoria. More th[an] 3,000 objects are on sh[ow,] some in their original surroundings by way of restored period rooms. Also sculpture, photogr[aphy] and paintings.

★ Brompton Oratory (G C2)

→ Brompton Rd, SW7
Daily 6.30am–8pm
This Baroque Catholic church (1804) houses 12 statues of the apost[les] by Mazzuoli (1644–172[?]) which once stood in th[e]

Map F

OLD BROMPTON RD

REDC

CHELSEA
SQUARE
BRITTEN ST
DOVEHOUSE ST

SOUTH PARADE
ST PETERS
ELM PLACE

STEVENS GDNS
ROLAND GDNS
ROLAND WAY

DRAYTON GDNS
CRESSWELL PL
THE LITTLE B

OLD BROMPTON RD

GALE STREET
SYDNEY ST
SYDNEY PL

NEVILLE ST
FOULIS TER
ONSLOW GDNS

CRANLEY MEWS
CRANLEY GARDENS
ROLAND GDNS
ONSLOW GDNS
OLD CHURCH ST
SUMNER PL
BRECHIN PL

WETHERBY GDNS
BINA GARDENS
ROSARY GDNS
HEREFORD SQUARE
WETHERBY PLACE

BOLTON GARDENS
BRAMHAM GARDENS
COLLINGHAM GARDENS

IXWORTH PL

FULHAM PLACE
FULHAM ROAD

CHRISTIE'S ★

ONSLOW SQUARE
SUMNER PLACE
ONSLOW SQUARE

PELHAM CRES

BROMPTON RD

PELHAM ST

GREVILLE PLACE
CLAREVILLE STREET
GLOUCESTER ROAD
HARRINGTON GARDENS

KENSINGTON GARDENS

COLLINGHAM GARDENS
COURTFIELD GARDENS
COURTFIELD ROAD
BARKSTON GARDENS
COLLINGHAM PLACE

MICHI HOU

BROMPTON TERRACE
PELHAM PLACE
ALEXANDER PLACE
SOUTH TERRACE

SOUTH KENSINGTON

KENSINGTON RD
THURLOE ST
THURLOE SQUARE

BUTE ST
HARRINGTON RD

ASHBURN PLACE
ASHBURN GARDENS
COURTFIELD GARDENS

GLOUCESTER
ROAD

CROMWELL ROAD

CROMWELL ROAD

ISMAILI CENTRE

CROMWELL PLACE

QUEEN'S GATE

NATURAL
HISTORY
MUSEUM ★

ST STEPHEN'S

GRENVILLE PLACE
GRENVILLE PLACE

LEXHAM
GARDENS

2

BROMPTON RD

VICTORIA
& ALBERT
MUSEUM ★

SCIENCE
MUSEUM ★

EXHIBITION ROAD

AYRTON ROAD

QUEEN'S GATE PLACE

CORNWALL GARDENS
CORNWALL GARDENS

ELDON
ROAD

STANFORD ROAD

ENNISMORE GARDENS
ENNISMORE GDNS

WATTS WAY
PRINCE'S GARDENS
PRINCE CONSORT RD

CALLENDER RD
GLOUCESTER RD

QUEEN'S GATE
TERRACE

ELVASTON PLACE
QUEEN'S GATE PLACE

LAUNCESTON PLACE

COTTESMORE
GARDENS
VICTORIA GROVE
ALBAN'S GROVE

KENSINGTON
COURT

IMPERIAL COLLEGE
OF SCIENCE AND
TECHNOLOGY

CANNING PLACE
KENSINGTON
GATE

DE VERE GDNS

KNIGHTSBRIDGE

ENNISMORE R

ENNIS STRE
SQUARE
BRO

BREMNER
ROAD
KENSINGTON
GORE

ROYAL
ALBERT HALL

KENSINGTON GORE

HYDE
PARK GATE
PARK GATE

PALACE GATE

VICTORIA ROAD

KENSINGTON
COURT

1

NEW RIDE

HYD

ALBERT MEMORIAL ROAD

ALBERT
MEMORIAL

KENSINGTON GARDENS

THE FLOWER WALK

THE BROAD WALK

KENSINGTON ROAD

A

B

C

Photo captions

CHRISTIE'S

NATURAL HISTORY MUSEUM

SCIENCE MUSEUM

Take a stroll through an area that exudes stylish elegance: from South Kensington's world-class museums and on to Knightsbridge, epicenter of luxury shopping with Harrods and Sloane Street, the showcase of haute couture. Further east, embassies and aristocratic residences hide behind the impressive façades of Belgravia, a world away from the lively village atmosphere of Chelsea. Here you can give free rein to extravagant impulses in the boutiques and inviting cafés or enjoy a more economical stroll past antique stores and along the pretty streets which, before World War Two, were home to penniless and bohemian artists.

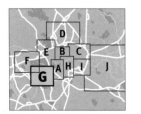

BIBENDUM

AMAYA

RESTAURANTS

Jenny Lo's Tea House (G F2)
→ 14 Eccleston St, SW1 Mon–Fri noon–3pm, 6–10pm; Sat 6–10pm
A wide variety of noodle and rice dishes in whimsical surroundings. Try the rice with eggplant in a Tuban soy sauce or seafood noodles with black beans. Dishes £8.

Pig's Ear (G C4)
→ 35 Old Church St, SW3 Tel. 020 7532 2908 Bar: daily noon–10pm (9.30pm Sun); upstairs: Mon–Fri 7pm–midnight; Sat 12.30–3.30pm, 7pm–midnight; Sun 12.30–4pm
A high-class gastropub serving beautifully prepared traditional food including roulade of black pudding with potato purée, lamb with haricot beans, and chocolate ice cream with shortbread, which diners eat either by candlelight in the ground floor bar or upstairs in the dining room. Dishes £17.

Cambio de Tercio (G A3)
→ 163 Old Brompton Rd, SW5; Tel. 020 7244 8970 Daily noon–2.30pm (3pm Sat-Sun), 7–11pm
The outspread capes of matadors adorn the walls of this warm and tempting restaurant. Mouthwatering choice of tapas for starters (clams, squid, Galician octopus) and perfect paellas. Excellent wine list. Reservation advisable at the weekend. Dishes £18.

Bibendum (G C2)
→ Michelin House, 81 Fulham Rd, SW3; Tel. 020 7581 5817 Daily noon–2.30pm (3pm Sat-Sun), 7–11pm (10pm Sun)
An old tire factory magnificently converted, with amazing Art Deco stained-glass windows. The oyster bar is cheaper than the restaurant but the latter's prices reflect Matthew Harris' excellent cuisine. Three courses set lunch £30 (restaurant).

Zafferano (G E1)
→ 15 Lowndes St, SW1 Tel. 020 7235 5800 Daily noon–2.30pm, 7–10.30pm
Very stylish, very accomplished genuine Italian fare by celebrated chef Giorgio Locatelli – tuna carpaccio with orange, fennel and mint, char grilled monkfish with zucchini and sweet chili, and some of the best pasta dishes you'll have ever tasted. The two- to four-course lunch menus (£29–£39) are very good value. Reserve well ahead.

Amaya (G E1)
→ 15 Halkin Arcade,

TUS BLUE   **ROYAL ALBERT HALL**   **CATH KIDSTON**

Motcomb St, SW1
Tel. 020 7823 1166
Daily 12.30–2.15pm, 6.30–
11.15pm (10.15pm Sun)
Sophisticated Indian
cuisine is served to a hip,
glamorous crowd in sultry
interiors decorated here
and there with a scattering
of rose petals. The menu
specializes in small
portions (kebabs), grilled
on the *sigiri*, or cooked in
the tandoor oven dishes.
The tiger prawn curry with
roast spices is particularly
good. Kebab £6–10,
menus £35–60 (8 to 11
courses).

Gordon Ramsay (E D4)
➔ 68-69 Royal Hospital
Square, SW3
Tel. 020 7352 4441; Mon-Fri
noon–2pm, 6.30–11pm
The enfant terrible of
British cooking may spend
a lot of his time doing TV
programs but dining in
Ramsay's first opened,
three Michelin-starred
Chelsea restaurant remains
an exceptional and
memorable experience –
coriander pappardelle
with baby clams, mussels
and chive velouté, sablé
Breton with marinated
figs, pistachio parfait and
spiced ice cream. Three-
course lunch menu £45.
Reserve no more than two
months in advance.

ICE CREAM PARLOR

Oddono's (G B2)
➔ 14 Bute St, SW7; Daily
11am–11pm (midnight Sat)
Fantastic Italian ice
creams: homemade, with
an unbeatable range of
flavors to choose from.

BARS, PUB, CONCERTS

Bistrot 190 (G B1)
➔ 190 Queen's Gate,
Gore Hotel, SW7
Daily 10am–midnight
The walls of this hotel
bar are covered with red
wood paneling and the
colonial-style decor, like
the sofas, encourage you
to sit back and take it
easy. Ideal for a drink
after a visit to one of the
many museums nearby.

Cactus Blue (G C3)
➔ 86 Fulham Rd, SW3
Mon-Sat 5pm–midnight;
Sun noon–11pm
A paradise for tequila
fans: there are dozens on
the menu, imported from
all over the world.

**The Anglesea
Arms** (G B3)
➔ 15 Selwood Terrace, SW7
Mon-Sat 11am–11pm;
Sun noon–10.30pm
A very English gastropub
with flowery Laura Ashley-
type wallpaper, glass and

wood partitions which
create small private areas,
and a terrace in spring
and summer. The food
isn't too expensive and
is consistently good.

Royal Albert Hall (G B1)
➔ Kensington Gore, SW7
Tel. 020 7838 3110
Tours (45 mins) 10.30am–
3.30pm (call to reserve)
The famous red-brick hall
owes its reputation to the
Proms, a series of classical
music concerts held each
summer, but it also stages
pop, classical, and jazz
concerts.

SHOPPING

Harrods (G D1)
➔ 87-135 Brompton Rd, SW1
Mon-Sat 10am–8pm;
Sun noon–6pm;
Founded by a tea
merchant, Henry Charles
Harrod in 1849, Harrods is
London's most legendary
store. The extraordinary
Food Halls are the main
attraction.

Harvey Nichols (G D1)
➔ Knightsbridge, SW1
Mon-Sat 10am–8pm;
Sun noon–6pm;
'Harvey Nics', however, is
more stylish and certainly
has the edge on Harrods
for designer collections.
Popular sushi bar on the
fifth floor.

The Pie Man (G D3)
➔ 16 Cale St, Chelsea Green,
SW3; Tel. 020 7225 0587
Mon-Fri 9am–5.30pm;
Sat 9.30am–2.30pm
As an alternative to
sandwiches, take out
some of these delicious
British dishes: lamb and
mint pie, salmon cake
or lemon cake.

**Chelsea Farmers
Market** (G C3)
➔ 125 Sydney St, SW3
A miniature market with
an eclectic mix of stores
in small, multicolored
wooden huts.

Cath Kidston (G B4)
➔ 322 King's Rd, SW3
Mon-Sat 10am–7pm; Sun
11am–5pm; other branches
Flowers, dots, strawberries
and stars are just some of
the brightly colored motifs
decorating picnic hampers,
household linens, fabrics,
clogs and gumboots.

Brora (G B4)
➔ 344 King's Rd, SW3
Mon-Sat 10am–6pm; Sun
noon–5pm; other branches
You don't often find
cashmere in that many
subtly blended shades,
something for which this
Scottish company is
renowned. Pullovers, hats
and cardigans in fresh
spring green, chocolate,
rosy apple and many
other colors.

…ORIA & ALBERT MUSEUM

BROMPTON ORATORY

K   D   E   F

SOUTH CARRIAGE DRIVE

HYDE PARK CORNER

LANESBOROUGH HOTEL

KNIGHTSBRIDGE

HARVEY NICHOLS

KNIGHTSBRIDGE

TREVOR STREET

TREVOR PLACE

RAPHAEL STREET

TREVOR SQUARE

MONTPELIER ST

LOWNDES SQUARE

KINNERTON ST

WILTON PLACE

WILTON CRES.

GROSVENOR CRESCENT

HALKIN STREET

HEADFORT PLACE

MONTROSE PL.

CHAPEL ST

PALACE GARDENS

GROSVENOR PLACE

ROYAL MEWS

LOWER GROSVENOR PL.

GROSVENOR GDNS

BROMPTON ROAD

SLOANE STREET

PAVILION ROAD

HANS CRES

BASIL ST

HANS RD

HALKIN ARCADE

MOTCOMB STREET

WEST HALKIN STREET

BELGRAVE SQUARE

CHESTER ST

BELGRAVE MEWS

UPPER BELGRAVE ST

WILTON ST

HARRODS

BASIL ST

BEAUFORT GARDENS

HANS PLACE

OVINGTON PL.

PONT STREET

PONT STREET

CADOGAN SQUARE

PAVILION ROAD

CHESHAM PLACE

BELGRAVE PL.

BELGRAVE SQUARE

BELGRAVIA

CHESHAM ST

LYALL STREET

EATON PL.

EATON SQUARE

ECCLESTON STREET

ST PETER'S

VICTORIA STATION

BEAUCHAMP PL.

OVINGTON GARDENS

…TON STREET

HASKER ST

FIRST ST

MOSSOP ST

DENYER ST

RAWINGS STREET

LENNOX GARDENS

MILNER STREET

MOORE STREET

HALSEY STREET

CADOGAN SQUARE

CADOGAN GATE

CADOGAN PLACE

CADOGAN LANE

EATON PLACE

EATON TERRACE

SOUTH EATON PL.

ELIZABETH STREET

CHESTER ROW

EATON SQUARE

CHESTER SQUARE

EBURY STREET

CHESTER SQ.

EBURY STREET

BUCKINGHAM PALACE ROAD

DRAYCOTT CADOGAN STREET

CADOGAN PLACE

HOLY TRINITY

CLIVEDEN PL.

ROYAL COURT THEATRE

CHESTER TERRACE

EATON TERRACE

SEMLEY PL.

VICTORIA COACH STATION

FOUNTAIN SQUARE

DRAYCOTT AVENUE

WHITEHEADS GROVE

DRAYCOTT PL.

BRAY PLACE

OSYMONS STREET

Sloane Square

SLOANE SQUARE

LOWER SLOANE ST

HOLBEIN PL.

BOURNE ST

EBURY ST

ST GEORGE'S DRIVE

ELYSTAN PLACE

KING'S ROAD

Duke of York's Sq.

SAATCHI GALLERY

CHELTENHAM TERRACE

PIMLICO ROAD

RANELAGH GROVE

WARWICK WAY

MARKHAM SQUARE

MARKHAM STREET

…JUBILEE PL.

WALPOLE ST

ROYAL AVENUE

TURKS ROW

FRANKLIN'S ROW

…COPY'S ST

SMITH ST

ST LEONARD'S TER.

CHELSEA BR

BURTON'S COURT

ROYAL

BRIDGE ROAD

SUTHERLAND STREET

CHELSEA

1

2

3

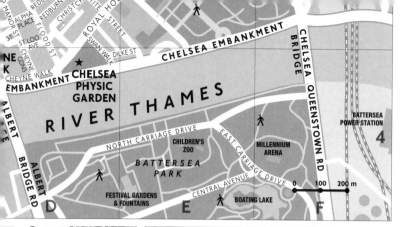

...L HOSPITAL

CHELSEA PHYSIC GARDEN

CHEYNE WALK

...edral in Siena, Italy.

...elgrave Square (G E1)
...haunt of robbers before ...s developed, this very ...rly district was ...gned in 1824 by ...mas Cubitt. Beautifully ...ortioned brick and ...e-stuccoed Victorian ...dings, so typical of ...sea, border the square.

...aatchi Gallery (G D3)
...ng's Rd, Duke of York's ...W3; Tel. 020 7823 2363 ...10am–6pm
...world's biggest private ...ry of contemporary art, ...nging to the immensely ...thy and controversial art ...ctor Charles Saatchi, ...ed last winter. A ...ering 70,000 square

feet of exhibition space in beautiful premises, it is dedicated to British modern art but also stages temporary exhibitions by contemporary foreign artists.

★ **Royal Hospital (G** E3)
→ Royal Hospital Rd, SW3 Tel. 020 7881 5200; Gardens: daily 10am (noon Sun)–8pm (4.30pm Oct-March; 7pm April, Sep); Mon-Sat 10am–noon, 2–4pm; Sun 2–4pm
The famous Chelsea Flower Show is held in May in the gardens of this army retirement home founded by Charles II in the 17th century. Its 400 Chelsea Pensioners, in 18th-century uniform, wear a tricorn hat on special occasions.

The chapel and refectory are open to visitors.

★ **Chelsea Physic Garden (G** D4)
→ 66 Royal Hospital Rd, SW3 Tel. 020 7352 5646; April-Oct: Wed-Fri noon–5pm (sunset Wed); Sun noon–6pm
The oldest botanical garden in England, along with that of Oxford, the Chelsea Physic Garden was founded in 1673 by the Apothecaries' Company, which wanted medicinal plants for scientific study. Through the centuries the garden grew more exotic species, thanks to gifts by, most notably, Sir Hans Sloane. Today there are more than 7,000 varieties of herbs,

fruits and vegetables, and many centenary trees.

★ **Cheyne Walk (G** D4)
Looking at the sober, elegant houses lining the street, you'd never think they had a rich intellectual and artistic history. But Henry James lived at no. 21, Dante Gabriel Rossetti, Algernon Swinburne and George Meredith all lived at no. 16, George Eliot died at no. 4 and Turner at no. 119. More recently, no. 48 used to belong to Rolling Stone Mick Jagger. The street has long lost its stately Victorian calm, although the ornate façades are still there as a reminder of its fascinating history.

BFI SOUTHBANK

ROYAL FESTIVAL HALL

VICTORIA TOWER GARDENS

MILLBANK

GDON ST

THORNEY STREET

MILLBANK TOWER

LAMBETH BRIDGE

ALBERT EMBANKMENT

LAMBETH PALACE ROAD

ALBERT EMB

LAMB

CARLISLE LA

ARCHBISHOPS PARK

LAMBETH PALACE

LAMBETH ROAD

PRATT WALK

SAIL ST

JUXON ST

OLD PARADISE STREET

LAMBETH HIGH ST

WHITGIFT STREET

BLACK

NEWPORT ST

LAMBETH WALK

GIBSON ROAD

LAMB

PRINCE

TYERS STREET

VAUXHALL WALK

CITADEL PLACE

JONATHAN STREET

VAUXHALL STREET

5

6

A   B

0   100   200 m

★ Blackfriars Bridge (H D1)
Beneath this colorful bridge with its surbased steel arches, a series of frescos illustrate the history of the surrounding area and the role played by the River Thames. The present structure dates from 1869, but a bridge has stood on this spot since 1769.
At that time it was the third to straddle the river: until 1738 London Bridge was the only bridge connecting the two banks.

★ Gabriel's Wharf (H C2)
→ 56 Upper Ground, SE1
Craft stores and boutiques, children's play area and café terraces. The little square and the few surrounding square yards would have ended up in the hands of a real estate developer, like the rest of the district, but for the tireless battle waged by the non-profit making Coin Street Community Builders.

★ National Theatre (H B2)
→ South Bank, SE1; Tel. 020 7452 3400; Mon-Sat 9.30am–11pm; guided tours (1¼ hrs) Mon-Sat: 10.15am, 12.15pm, 5.15pm (the latter not on Sat)
Although this may look like a fortress the National, as it is simply known, is one of the most acclaimed theaters in the city. Designed by Denys Lasdun in 1975, this concrete building has three auditoriums which stage everything from avant-garde plays to spectacular big-name musicals. Guided tours take you backstage for a fascinating look at the stage machinery (the tour starts in the main hall which mounts exhibitions of contemporary art).

★ BFI Southbank (H B2)
→ South Bank, SE1; Tel. 020 7928 3232; Daily 11am–11pm
Formerly known as the National Film Theatre, the British Film Institute is the temple of cinema in London, with three screens for movies, retrospectives and talks, and a library that holds the world's largest collection of information on film and television. Majo events are organized su as the London Film Fest which screens internatio movies in the fall. The B IMAX cinema, which has UK's largest movie scree is close by (E C3).

★ South Bank Centre (H B2)
→ Belvedere Rd, South Ba SE1; Tel. 08703 800400 Daily 11am–11pm
The controversy (its criti felt that the chilly gray concrete shouldn't have been left without adornment) that surroun this artistic center after construction in 1951 has now more or less died down. A recent major

H

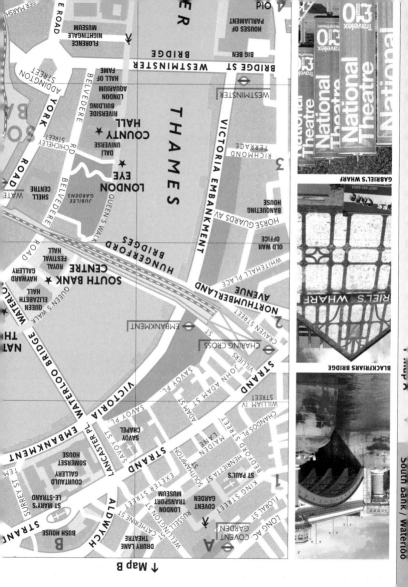

There are few surviving vestiges of this area's past; the swamps were drained centuries ago and the last war decimated the factories and workshops which, in the 19th century, had transformed these villages into an important industrial center. The land on the south bank was subsequently cleared of rubble to build cultural facilities capable of rivaling those on the north bank. The South Bank Arts Centre, completed in the 1960s, was the first building in this complex and many others have been built since. Queen's Walk now extends west alongside the river. The promenade affords stunning views of the buildings across the water and, on fine days, a stroll from the London Eye to Tower Bridge is a real pleasure.

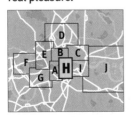

LIVEBAIT

THE BLACK FRIAR

RESTAURANTS

Meson Don Felipe (H D3)
→ 53 The Cut, SE1
Tel. 020 7928 3237
Mon–Sat noon–11pm
A first-class tapas bar serving the usual small-sized portions of Spanish delicacies – light and tasty. The place is packed and noisy in the evening, with flamenco guitarists playing most nights. Very good wines at very good value. Tapas from £3.95.

Laughing Gravy (H D3)
→ 154 Blackfriars Rd, SE1
Tel. 020 7721 7055
Mon–Fri noon–11pm
A homely, quiet bar-gastropub, where many locals hang out because the food is spot on and – almost – reasonably priced. Try the incredibly tender bison (signature dish). Belgian beers and Breton cider. Dishes £7.50 (bar); £22 (restaurant).

Anchor & Hope (H D3)
→ 36 The Cut, SE1
Tel. 020 7928 9898
Mon 6–10.30pm; Tue-Sat noon–2.30pm, 6–10.30pm
The gastropub of the south bank, co-founded by two chefs who learned their skills at St John (see **C**), among other places. Adventurous, changing menu of a rather rich

cuisine: snail and bacon salad, lamb gnocchi with olives and lentils. Simple decor of wooden tables and chairs. No bookings taken so you may have to wait in the bar area, especially at the weekend. Dishes £14.

Livebait (H D3)
→ 43 The Cut, SE1
Tel. 020 7928 7211; Mon-Sat noon–11pm; Sun 12.30–9pm
A white-and-green tiled seafood restaurant whose fish, fresh from the day's market, and friendly ambience have been a winning formula since it opened in 1998. Dishes are of the utmost simplicity along with some clever combinations, such as tuna with a soy and honey marinade. Dishes £11–18; pre-theater menu £14.50.

Baltic (H D3)
→ 74 Blackfriars Rd, SE1
Tel. 020 7928 1111
Mon-Sat noon–3pm, 6–11pm; Sun noon–11pm
It has a long, seductive bar, a vast dining room with a glass roof supported by oak beams, and a modernist, gray decor that can seem rather cold – somewhat less so once you've tried some of the 40 types of vodka on offer. Fantastic Polish and modern Eastern-European

ANA

KONDITOR & COOK

WHAT THE BUTLER WORE

food – marinated herrings with cucumber, potato and dill salad; paprika chicken with spiced bean salad and garlic yogurt. The desserts are also very good. Live jazz every Sun from 7pm. Dishes £7.50 (bar); £17 (restaurant).

BARS, PUBS, CLUB, GAMES

OXO Tower Bar (H C2)
→ OXO Tower, 8th floor, SE1
Tel. 020 7803 3888; Mon-Sat 11am–midnight (11pm Mon-Wed); Sun noon–10pm
This floor of the OXO tower offers exhilarating views of the Thames and north bank, especially in the evening when the sky is clear. Have a drink at the bar amidst a mix of City suits and romantic couples, then go down to the second floor to the Japanese yakitori restaurant Bincho.

Gordon's Wine Bar (H A2)
→ 47 Villiers St, WC2
Mon-Sat 10am (11am Sat)–11pm; Sun noon–10pm
Located in the depths of an ancient cellar that echoes to the sound of conversation rather than music, this historic bar has only bottles for decoration. There are over

1,000 vintages to taste in this long, candlelit room – or outside on the grass in Embankment Park.

The Black Friar (H D1)
→ 174 Queen Victoria St, EC4
Tel. 020 7236 5474; Daily 10am (11am Sat- Sun)–11pm
Mosaics, polychrome marble and carved monks of all sizes decorate this fantastic Arts and Crafts pub, famous for its extravagant decor.

Cubana (H C3)
→ 48 Lower Marsh, SE1
Mon-Fri noon–midnight (3am-Fri); Sat 5pm–3am
This bar will brighten your spirits in any weather. Religious trinkets, brightly-colored chairs, portraits of Che and photos of Cuba adorn the walls against a background of Latino rhythms. The two bars serve cocktails, wine, bottled beer and tapas. Salsa: Wed 10.30pm–12.30am; Thu 11pm–1am; Fri-Sat 11pm–3am.

Heaven (H A2)
→ Under the arches in Villiers St, WC2; Mon, Wed, Fri-Sat 11pm–6am
Beneath the rail track at Charing Cross are drag queens, topless barmen, and gogo dancers in an ear-splittingly loud techno labyrinth that is very

popular with the gay set.

Namco Play Station (H B3)
→ Riverside Building, County Hall, SE1
Daily 10am–midnight
A modern paradise for devotees of video games and simulators, with eight billiard tables, a bowling alley, and giant screens. Try your hand at the latest game or race around in the fastest bumper cars in Europe.

SHOPPING

Konditor & Cook (H C3)
→ 22 Cornwall Rd, SE1
Tel. 020 7261 0456
Mon-Fri 7.30am–6.30pm; Sat 8am–3pm; also in Borough Market and inside The Gherkin (C E3)
Just a few minutes away from Waterloo Station this patisserie is well worth a detour for its fantastic range of exquisitely made cakes and buns, from humble scones to the gorgeous whisky and orange gateau.

What the Butler Wore (H C4)
→ 131 Lower Marsh, SE1
Tel. 020 7261 1353
Mon-Sat 11am–6pm
A small, second-hand clothes store for lovers of 1960s and 1970s garb.

Everything is in excellent condition and, given the number of revivals, usually looks bang up-to-date.

Gramex (H C4)
→ 25 Lower Marsh, SE1
Tel. 020 7401 3830
Mon-Sat 11am–7pm
A key attraction for lovers of classical music, some of whom come to sit and snooze in the comfy chairs at the back of the store. Vinyl, second-hand CDs, and expert advice.

OXO Tower Design Shops (H C2)
→ OXO Tower Wharf, Barge House St, SE1
Tue-Sun 11am–6pm
The restored Art Deco Oxo Tower Wharf now houses a complex of shops-cum-workshops belonging to independent designers, some of whom sell their designs here exclusively. Hand-woven silk, jewelry, children's clothes, porcelain and small pieces of furniture.

Ganesha (H C2)
→ 3 Gabriel's Wharf, SE1
Daily noon–6pm
Cushions, tunics, bags and accessories in a boutique that celebrates Indian culture and craftsmanship, while promoting the crucial importance of fairtrade products.

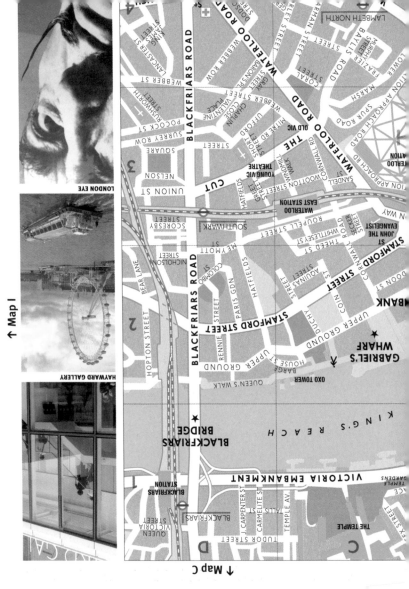

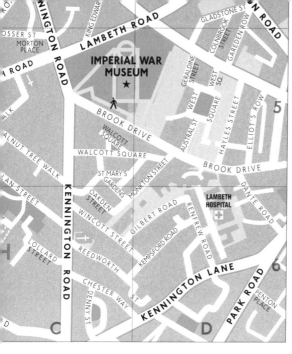

LONDON AQUARIUM

IMPERIAL WAR MUSEUM

ram of renovation has
o the opening of many
urants and cafés along
mbankment to make
South Bank more
oming. Visitors,
ever, never ceased
ing to the concert hall,
vated by its vast
or spaces flooded
light. It's worth a visit
g the day to listen to
e lunchtime concert, or
nply relax and enjoy
nk looking at the river.

l Festival Hall
t concert hall with
otional acoustics and
erb program of jazz,
ical, rock and pop.

ell Room
aller hall for recitals

and chamber music, again
with excellent acoustics.
Queen Elizabeth Hall
Dance and classical music.
Hayward Gallery
→ *Daily 10am–6pm
(8pm Fri-Sat)*
Major painting, sculpture
and photography
exhibitions are shown in
this stark concrete gallery,
to which a glass pavilion
designed by New York-
based artist Dan Graham
was added in 2003.
★ London Eye (H B3)
→ *Queen's Walk SE1
Tel. 0870 5000 600; Daily
10am–9pm (8pm Oct-May);
reservation recommended*
Take a 40-minute trip on the
tallest wheel in the world.

From a height of 443 ft you
enjoy (in good weather!)
spectacular views over
London. On a clear day you
can see for 25 miles.
★ County Hall (H B3)
→ *Riverside Building,
County Hall, SE1*
Dalí Universe
→ *Tel. 020 7620 2720
Daily 9.30am–6.30pm*
A museum opened in 2004
for the centenary of Dalí's
birth, and entirely devoted
to him. With 500 of his
works (drawings, objects,
sculptures) arranged
thematically within three
sections (Sensuality and
Femininity, Religion and
Mythology and Dreams and
Fantasy), this makes for a

fascinating journey into the
mind of the Surrealist artist.
London Aquarium
→ *Tel. 020 7967 8000
Daily 10am–6pm*
Stroke the rays, watch
the sharks being fed and
discover fresh-water and
salt-water fish from all
over the world.
**★ Imperial War
Museum (H** C5)
→ *Lambeth Rd, SE1
Tel. 020 7416 5000
Daily 10am–6pm*
An unrivalled collection
of war memorabilia. In the
basement, special attention
is paid to the two World
Wars; the upper floors are
given over to a very moving
study of the Holocaust.

LONDON DUNGEON

SOUTHWARK CATHEDRAL

SHAKESPEARE'S GLOBE EXHIBITION

★ **Tower of London** (**I** E1)
→ Tower Hill EC3
Tel. 08707 567 070; Daily 9am
(10am Sun-Mon)–6pm
William the Conqueror built
the tower to ensure control
of the river. The
impregnable fortress was
also used as a jail: famous
prisoners here have
included Anne Boleyn,
Guy Fawkes, and Rudolf
Hess. Today the tower no
longer strikes terror into
people's hearts but the
Yeomen Warders, in Tudor
costume, continue to mount
guard. The fabulous Crown
Jewels are used in coronations
are on show here, and
there is an important
collection of armour.

★ **Design Museum** (**I** F2)
→ 28 Shad Thames SE1
Tel. 020 7940 8790
Daily 10am–5.45pm
Devoted to the study of
design for mass production
with two floors of temporary
exhibitions on technological
advances and design trends.
Examples of everyday items
such as washing machines,
telephones, cameras
radios, and chairs are
testament to the esthetic
revolutions heralded by the
industrial era.

★ **Tower Bridge** (**I** F1)
→ Tel. 020 7403 3761
Daily 10am–6.30pm (9.30am–
6pm in Oct-March)
As much a symbol of
London as Big Ben, the
distinctive silhouette of
Tower Bridge evokes the
Victorian era when England
was a powerful seafaring
nation. River traffic was
extremely heavy at that time
and the movable bridges
were raised to allow ships
to pass through. The two
neo-Gothic towers conceal
the complex hydraulic lifting
machinery used to raise the
two 1,000-ton bascules.
A museum recounts the
history of the bridge.

★ **HMS *Belfast*** (**I** D1)
→ Morgan's Lane SE1
Tel. 020 7940 6300; Daily
10am–6pm (5pm Nov-Feb)
Experience the life of a
sailor on board a warship.
This one was in service

from 1938 to the end
of the Korean War in 195
★ **Hay's Wharf** (**I** D1)
In the 19th century,
merchant ships were
loaded and unloaded a
the bustling quays of the
Thames. The two impres
red brick and light stone
buildings were once use
as warehouses for storin
butter and spices. They
connected by a passage
with a glazed barrel vau
supported by a slender
steel framework which
soars to a height of 98
Innovatively renovated
Twigg, Brown & Partner
in the 1980s, the Hay's
Galleria now houses ca
restaurants and stores.

I

TOWER OF LONDON

TOWER BRIDGE

A ★ MILLENNIUM BRIDGE B

SHAKESPEARE'S GLOBE EXHIBITION

BANKSIDE

★ TATE MODERN

★ NEW GLOBE WALK

WALBROOK WHARF

WATERMAN'S WALK

FISHMONGE HALL

SOUTHWARK BRIDGE

BANKSIDE

BANK END

LONDON BRIDGE C

HOPTON STREET

HOLLAND ST

PARK STREET

EMERSON STREET

PARK STREET

VINOPOLIS

CATHEDRAL STREET

GOLDEN HINDE

CLINK STREET

SUMNER STREET

GREAT GUILDFORD ST

SUMNER ST

ZOAR ST

SOUTHWARK

SOUTHWARK BRIDGE ROAD

PARK ST

WINCHESTER WK

MONTAGUE CLO.

★ SOUTHWARK CATHEDRAL

SOUTHWARK STREET

BURRELL ST

CHANCEL ST

GAMBIA ST

GT SUFFOLK ST

LAVINGTON ST

EWER ST

MAIDEN LANE

THRALE ST

STONEY ST

BOROUGH MARKET

LONDON B ST

OLD T

DOLBEN ST

UNION STREET

UNION STREET

UNION STREET

RED CROSS WAY

AYRES ST

BOROUGH

HIGH STREET

GUY'S HOSPITAL

GREAT MAZE P

NELSON SQUARE

GREAT SUFFOLK STREET

COPPERFIELD STREET

LOMAN ST

SAWYER ST

POCOCK ST

MARSHALSEA RD

LITTLE DORRIT COURT

NEWCOMEN STREET

MERMAID CT

CROSBY ROW

PORLO ST

SN

SURREY ROW

POCOCK ST

KINGS BENCH ST

GLASSHILL STREET

RUSHWORTH ST

SUDREY ST

BITTERN ST

LANT STREET

TOMLIN ST

SOUTHWARK BRIDGE ROAD

BOROUGH

ST GEORGE

LONG LANE

WEBBER STREET

LIBRARY STREET

LANCASTER ST

KING JAMES STREET

GREAT SUFFOLK ST

SCOVELL ROAD

STONES END STREET

BOROUGH

SWAN ST

COLE ST

TABARD ST

GREAT DOVER S

PILGRIMAGE ST

GLOBE ST

TAB

MAN C

TABARD

TRINITY S ST

BOROUGH ROAD

Southwark had always been London's poor relation and, with its brothels, taverns and theaters, a dumping ground for unwanted people and pastimes. The docks ushered in a period of prosperity but the district suffered anew when they were closed in 1950. Various new projects and restoration programs followed after the Design Museum opened in 1989, culminating in the inauguration of the Tate Modern in May 2000. The two are linked by Queen's Walk, a very pleasant riverside path. Wealthier people have taken up residence in the area, but further south are still some of the capital's least fashionable districts.

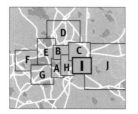

BERMONDSEY KITCHEN

FISH!

RESTAURANTS

M. Manze (I E3)
→ 87 Tower Bridge Rd, SE1
Tue-Sat 10.30am (10am Fri-Sat)–2pm; Mon 11am–2pm
The hearty meal of 'pie, eels and mash' exemplifies London's culinary traditions but is rarely found on a menu nowadays. Take out or eat in the 100-year-old canteen-like restaurant, which is as much an attraction as the food. £3.

El Vergel (I B2)
→ 8 Lant St, SE1
Tel. 020 7357 0057; Mon-Sat 8am (10.30am)–3pm
A colorful Latin-American deli, five minutes from Borough subway station. Sandwiches, Mexican salads (£5) and first-class service. Specialty: torta mexicana sandwich with chicken, beans, and guacamole.

Tapas Brindisa (I C2)
→ 18-20 Southwark St
Borough Market; Mon-Sat 11am–11pm; Spanish breakfast Fri-Sat 9–11am
The Brindisa store has been a staple of Borough market for 20 years, famous for importing high-quality Spanish fare. A tapas bar round the corner using their produce (their charcuterie is

second to none) and that of the farmers and fishermen on sale at Borough was bound to be a success. Lively, noisy, friendly. They have just opened Tierra Brindisa at 46 Broadwick St, Soho (**B** B3). Tapas £3.95–6.50.

Tas Pide (I B1)
→ 20-22 New Globe Walk, SE1; Tel. 020 7928 3300; Daily noon–11.30pm (10.30pm Sun)
Interesting, tasty Anatolian (Turkish) cuisine and pide, a sort of pizza dough in the shape of a boat, baked on site and garnished with mouthwatering ingredients – the pide with grilled sardines wrapped in vine leaves, onions, olives and lemon zest is delicious. Menus from £8.75.

Bermondsey Kitchen (I D3)
→ 194 Bermondsey St, SE1
Tel. 020 7407 5719; Mon-Fri noon–3pm, 6.30–10.30pm; Sat-Sun 9.30am–3.30pm
Dine around the central kitchen in this bright space; relaxed, friendly and filled with locals at the weekend. The seasonal menu changes daily and much of its produce comes from Borough Market. Tapas and brunch at weekends. Dishes £13.50.

Kwan Thai (I D1)
→ The Riverfront Hay's Wharf;

OPOLIS WINE WHARF

BOROUGH MARKET

NEAL'S YARD DAIRY

Tel. 020 7403 7373
*Mon-Fri noon–3pm,
6–10.30pm, Sat 6–10.30pm*
A first-class Thai restaurant with a terrace looking out over the City across the river. Subtly flavored cuisine, with superb green and red curries with lemongrass. Dishes £15.

Delfina (I D2**)**
→ *Bermondsey St, SE1
Tel. 020 7357 0244; Mon-Fri noon–3pm (and 7–10pm Fri)*
For many years the canteen of the artists in residence, this light, airy spot has blossomed to become a restaurant in its own right. A surprising, eclectic modern menu changes fortnightly: pan-fried sea bass with artichoke puree and spiced roast pears; coffee roasted ostrich steak. Dishes £16.

Fish! (I C1**)**
→ *Cathedral St, SE1
Tel. 020 7407 3803
Mon-Thu 11.30am–11pm;
Fri-Sun noon–11pm*
With its steel and glass structure, it looks very much like an aquarium. The delicious dishes depend on the daily deliveries: squid, fresh cod, skate, swordfish – grilled or steamed. Dishes £16.

CAFÉ

**Maria's Market
Café (I** C2**)**
→ *Borough Market;
Wed-Sat 5.45am–3pm (5pm
Thu; 6pm Fri; 4pm Sat)*
If your heart is set on a traditional English breakfast, this café, deep in the heart of Borough, is one of the best. Not exactly fat-free but there are lighter alternatives.

BAR, PUBS, CLUB

**Vinopolis
Wine Wharf (I** C1**)**
→ *Stoney St, SE1
Tel. 020 7940 8335
Mon-Sat noon–11.30pm*
A huge wine bar under the high brick arches of an old bridge, with a list of over 300 vintages sold by the glass. There is a more intimate tapas bar tucked away in a recess.

The Anchor (I B1**)**
→ *34 Park St, SE1
Mon-Sat 11am–midnight;
Sun noon–11pm*
Built in 1770, this old pub was recently given a face lift. In summer the large terrace with wooden tables is perfect for enjoying a drink in the sunshine. Docked just outside the pub is the 16th-century *Golden Hinde*.

George Inn (I C2**)**
→ *77 Borough High St, SE1
Mon-Sat 11am–11pm;
Sun noon–10.30pm*
This listed building dating from 1676 is London's only surviving galleried coaching inn. There is a restaurant upstairs in the former bedrooms and some cute little rooms at street level that can only be entered from the pretty cobbled courtyard.

**Ministry
of Sound (I** A3**)**
→ *103 Gaunt St, SE1
Tel. 020 7740 8600; Fri-Sat
11pm–6am (7am Sat)*
More than a nightclub, the Ministry is a brand and a legend with an exceptional sound system. Three dance floors play techno, garage, and house music.

SHOPPING

Borough Market (I C2**)**
→ *London Bridge, SE1
Thu 11am–5pm; Fri noon–
6pm; Sat 9am–4pm*
The oldest food market in London (1756) and one that chefs seem to like best. Under the railway lines, behind Southwark Cathedral, stalls and small stores sell mostly organic produce – spices (try the smoked paprika

sold in the Brindisa store), meat, fish, cheese, oils, bread, cakes, and more.

Neal's Yard Dairy (I B2**)**
→ *6 Park St, SE1
Tel. 020 7367 0799; Mon-Fri
9am–6pm; Sat 8am–5pm*
Shelves from floor to ceiling are piled with maturing wheels of farmhouse cheeses.

**The Christmas
Shop (I** D1**)**
→ *55A Hay's Galleria, Tooley
St, SE1; Mon-Fri 8.30am–
6pm; Sat-Sun 10.30am–5pm*
A space devoted to beautiful and original Christmas decorations.

**Bermondsey
Market (I** E3**)**
→ *Bermondsey St, SE1
Fri 4am–1pm*
Each Friday antique stalls spread through the streets of this district, which is full of second-hand furniture stores. The market is frequented by many dealers – proof that there are bargains to be had if you're an early riser.

Vinopolis (I B1**)**
→ *1 Bank End St
Tel. 020 7940 8300
Mon-Fri noon–10pm; Sat
11am–9pm; Sun noon–6pm*
For a fascinating tour round the world of wine, with tasting. Guided tours available on request.
£19.50–32.50.

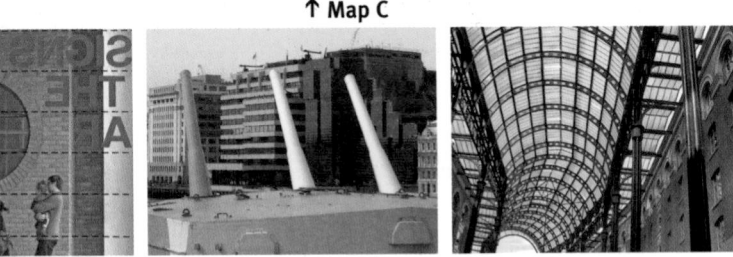

GN MUSEUM

HMS BELFAST

HAY'S WHARF

D
E TOWER HILL
F ROYAL MINT
DOCK ST

LOWER THAMES BYWARD TOWER STREET

OLD BILLINGSGATE MARKET
CUSTOM HOUSE

EAST SMITHFIELD

TOWER OF LONDON
★

TOWER BR. APPROACH

WORLD TRADE CENTRE

IVORY HOUSE

1

RIVER

BASIN

THAMES

ST KATHARINE'S WAY

HMS BELFAST ★

QUEEN'S ★ WALK

HAY'S WHARF

TOWER BRIDGE
★

COUNTER ST

TOOLEY

CITY HALL

QUEEN'S WALK

UPPER

LONDON DUNGEON

MORGAN'S LANE

POOL

LONDON BRIDGE STATION

ABBOTS LANE
VINE LANE
WEAVER'S LANE

SHAD THAMES

HORSELYDOWN LA

ST

HOLYROOD ST

POTTERS FIELDS

GAINSFORD STREET

DESIGN MUSEUM
★

2

TOOLEY STREET

BARNHAM STREET

LAFONE STREET

CURLEW STREET

STREET

QUEEN ELIZABETH STREET

MELIOR ST

WESTON STREET

SNOWSFIELDS

CRUCIFIX LANE

DRUID STREET

TOOLEY STREET

SHAD THAMES

KIRBY GRO.

TOWER BRIDGE ROAD

JAMAICA ROAD

TYERS GATE

WHITES GROUNDS

BERMONDSEY STREET

WESTON STREET

LEATHERMARKET GARDENS

LEATHERMARKET ST

BRUNSWICK COURT

TANNER STREET

MILL STREET

MOROCCO

STREET

BERMONDSEY STREET

DRUID STREET

SWEENEY CRESCENT

G LANE

BERMONDSEY

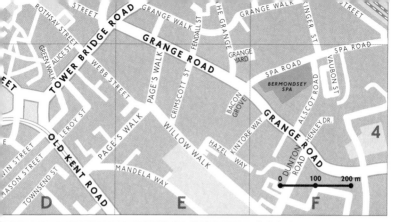

The map shows streets including ROTHSAY STREET, STREET, GRANGE WALK, FENDALL ST, THE GRANGE, GRANGE WALK, STREET, GRANGE ROAD, GRANGE YARD, SPA ROAD, VAUBAN ST, TOWER BRIDGE ROAD, WEBB STREET, PAGE'S WALK, CRIMSCOTT ST, BACON GROVE, BERMONDSEY SPA, ALSCOT ROAD, HENLEY DR., GREENWALK, ALICE ST, LEROY ST, OLD KENT ROAD, WIN STREET, MASON STREET, TOWNSEND ST, PAGE'S WALK, WILLOW WALK, MANDELA WAY, HAZEL WALK, KINTORE WAY, DUNTON ROAD, GRANGE ROAD

0   100   200 m

D   E   F

4

MODERN

2000

MILLENNIUM BRIDGE

---

ndon

geon (I D2)

-34 Tooley St, SE1

20 7403 7221

10am–5.30pm

rific tour based on

le events and crimes in

ountry's history. The

ncludes waxworks,

ky corridors, ghastly

eons and the chance to

ed, sentenced to death

nanged. No admittance

ldren under 10 years.

uthwark

edral (I C1)

ntague Close, SE1

8am–6pm

of the few vestiges of

strict's medieval past,

m Shakespeare's

er Edmund is buried

here. The church has been remodeled on many occasions but the current building retains the choir and the ambulatory of the Gothic church (1273). The triforium was inspired by the cathedrals of Chartres and Reims in France. There is a fine recumbent statue of a knight made of carved oak (13th century).

★ **Shakespeare's Globe Exhibition** (I B1)

→ New Globe Walk, SE1

Tel. 020 7902 1500; Daily

10am–5pm (9am–12.30pm,

1–5pm in April-Sep)

A museum charting the epic reconstruction of the Globe, Shakespeare's theater. Ten years in the making, it was

built close to the original site, using 17th-century materials and techniques.

★ **Tate Modern** (I A1)

→ Bankside, SE1

Tel. 020 7887 8000; Daily

10am–6pm (10pm Fri-Sat)

The splendid achievement of architects Herzog and De Meuron finally gave London an international museum of modern art. Stripped of its boilers and turbines, the 1947 power station now has 100,000 square feet of galleries arranged thematically, which house the whole of the Tate's collection of modern art. The Turbine Hall soars to a height of 115 ft and functions as a reception

and temporary exhibitions area. Extremely well-stocked bookstore. The restaurant on the top floor affords great views over St Paul's and the Thames.

★ **Millennium Bridge** (I A1)

→ Across from Tate Modern

The first bridge to be built in London for over a century closed for two years two days after its opening (2000) due to wobbling. Today the steel foot suspension bridge, designed by Norman Foster and Partners in collaboration with sculptor Anthony Caro, safely links the south bank with St Paul's.

THE QUEEN'S HOUSE

OLD ROYAL OBSERVATORY

RANGER'S HOUSE

★ Canary Wharf (J D2)

By the late 1980s the London Docks were nearing the end of their active life and developers were able to acquire large areas that were rapidly becoming a wasteland. The extension of the Jubilee Line in 1993 made it possible for large City companies to move their headquarters here, to a maze of streets and underground walkways at the foot of skyscrapers. At the exit of the Underground station designed by Norman Foster (1999) stands Cesar Pelli's 771-ft tower One Canada Square (1991), covered with stainless steel and dazzling in the sunlight.

★ Museum in Docklands (J D2)

→ *1 Warehouse, West India Quay, E14; Tel. 08704 443 856 Daily 10am–5.30pm*

A disused 18th-century warehouse converted into a museum explaining the fascinating history of the Port of London, whose activity dominated the region. There are Roman and Viking remains, model ships, descriptions of the slave trade, and a reconstructed Victorian street complete with sound effects.

★ Island Gardens (J E3)

→ *Elevators down to tunnel: Mon–Sat 7am–7pm; Sun 10am–5.30pm*

South of the Isle of Dogs is a small garden that offers the best view of Greenwich. To reach it, take the pedestrian tunnel under the river that was opened in 1897.

★ Old Royal Naval College (J E4)

→ *Painted Hall and Chapel open daily 10am–5pm*

The superb collection of four buildings that comprise the Naval College include two baroque masterpieces by Wren on the south side. The fine Painted Hall in is the west wing, covered in trompe-l'oeil motifs by Thornhill. Facing it stands the Chapel of St Peter and St Paul, richly decorated by James 'Athenian' Stuart.

★ National Maritime Museum (J E4)

→ *Park Row, SE10; Tel. 020 8858 4422; Daily 10am–5p*

A magnificent naval museum, beautifully lai around a glazed courtya with rooms devoted to explaining the conquest the Empire, polar exploration, life on boa the great liners, and mo Look out for the beautif state barge (1732) of Frederick, Prince of Wal

★ The Queen's House (J E4)

→ *Park Row, SE10; Tel. 020 8312 6693; Daily 10am–5p*

The first classical buildi be constructed in Engla (Inigo Jones, 1616), this

CANARY WHARF

MUSEUM IN DOCKLANDS

Map C

A   B   C

HACKNEY RD
COLUMBIA RD
OLD ST
SHOREDITCH HIGH STREET
GREAT EASTERN ST
WARNER PL
EZRA ST
COLUMBIA RD
GOSSET ST
POLLARD ROW
OLD BETHNAL GREEN ROAD
OLD FORD RD
ROMAN ROAD
TREBEC

V&A MUSEUM OF CHILDHOOD

BETHNAL GREEN
MEATH GARDENS
GROVE ROAD
MILE END PARK
MILE END
MILE

1

WORSHIP ST
SHOREDITCH
CHESHIRE ST
BRICK LANE
QUAKER ST
DRAY WALK
HANBURY ST
BUXTON ST
BETHNAL GARDENS
CAMBRIDGE HEATH RD
GLOBE ROAD
STEPNEY GREEN
BURDETT ROAD
BOW
MILE END PARK
ST PAUL'S

BETHNAL GREEN
VALLANCE ROAD
WHITECHAPEL

LIVERPOOL STATION
BISHOPS GATE
SPITALFIELDS
COMMERCIAL ST
WHITECHAPEL ROAD
MILE END ROAD
STEPNEY GREEN
WHITEHORSE LANE
STEPNEY
NEW RD
STEPNEY WAY
SIDNEY STREET
STEPNEY WAY
STEPNEY GREEN
BEN JONSON RD

LEADENHALL ST
FENCHURCH ST
ALDGATE
CANNON ST
COMMERCIAL ROAD
RATCLIFFE
SALMON LANE
LIMEHOUSE ROA

2

TOWER HILL
BYWARD ST
TOWER OF LONDON
MINORIES
PRESCOT STREET
EAST SMITHFIELD
DLR TOWER GATEWAY
CABLE STREET
SHADWELL DLR
CABLE STREET
WHITECHAPEL
THE HIGHWAY
DLR LIMEHOUSE
LIMEHOUSE
LIMEHOUSE LIN
LIMEHOUSE TUNNEL

TOWER BRIDGE
ST KATHARINE'S WAY
BUTLERS WHARF
SHAD THAMES
THE HIGHWAY
TOBACCO DOCK
WAPPING LANE
SHADWELL
KING EDWARD MEMORIAL PARK
WAPPING HYDRAULIC POWER STATION
WAPPING WALL
WAPPING
ROTHERHITHE STREET
CANA

TOOLEY ST
DESIGN MUSEUM
WAPPING
WAPPING HIGH ST
ROTHERHITHE
SALTER ROAD
ECOLOGICAL PARK

ST THOMAS STREET
DRUID ST
BERMONDSEY
BRUNEL RD
RUSSIA DOCK WOODLAND
SALTER ROAD

TOWER BRIDGE ROAD
ABBEY ST
GRANGE RD
JAMAICA RD
BERMONDSEY
SOUTHWARK PARK
CANADA WATER
LOWER ROAD
ROTHERHITHE
CRIFF ROAD
GREENLAND

As the Thames meanders eastward, both sides of the river show the shape of things to come. On the south bank, buoyed up by the success of Canary Wharf, are the former docks with rows of warehouses undergoing conversion as far as the Millennium Dome O2, a vast arena on an isolated spit of land. From the Isle of Dogs, once home to the kennels of King Henry VIII, the Thames can be crossed on foot to reach the old town of Greenwich, whose park is bisected by the Meridian Line. On the north side is the former working-class district of Bethnal Green, now busy with trendy boutiques and the glitzy bars of Brick Lane, one of the latest streets to become fashionable.

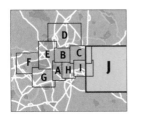

PAVILION TEA HOUSE

E. PELLICCI

RESTAURANTS

Pavilion
Tea House (J E4)
→ *Greenwich Park Blackheath Gate, SE10*
Tel. 020 8858 9695
Daily 9am–4pm or 5.30pm according to season
After the stiff climb up to the Observatory, relax in this small octagonal pavilion selling hot food, soups, salads, scones and sandwiches. The outside terrace has fine views of the park.
Dishes £6.

E. Pellicci (J B1)
→ *332 Bethnal Green Rd, E2; Tel. 020 7739 4873*
Mon-Sat 6.15am–4.45pm
An Italian restaurant in a working-class part of the city, family-run for three generations. Terrific home cooking in a tiny wood-paneled dining-room where diners share a table to eat a hearty English breakfast, pasta, or steak and fries. Dishes £6.

Royal China (J D2)
→ *30 West Ferry Circus, E14*
Tel. 020 7719 0888
A Chinese institution with three other branches in London, known for its excellent dim sum (served from noon to 5pm) and this Canary Wharf address, with Royal China's trademark black-lacquered interior, doesn't belie the reputation. Reserve at the weekend in good weather to secure a table under the trees. Brisk service. Dim sum £3; dishes £8–12.

Wapping Food (J B2)
→ *Wapping Hydraulic Power Station, E1; Tel. 020 7680 2080; Mon-Fri noon–3.30pm, 6.30–11pm; Sat 10am–4pm, 7–11pm; Sun 10am–4pm*
A defunct power station that doubles as an art gallery and now serves great food too, including salmon risotto, salt cod brandade, and roast chicken with angel-hair fries in the best tradition of modern British cuisine.
Dishes £17.

Café Spice
Namasté (J A2)
→ *16 Prescot St, E1*
Tel. 020 7488 9242; Mon-Fri noon–3pm, 6.15–10.30pm; Sat 6.15–10.30pm
The spectacular Gothic decor reinterpreted *à la* Bollywood, with sumptuous draped fabrics, won't leave you indifferent. The cuisine, however, is superb and comes from all over the subcontinent: Punjab, Rajasthan, Kashmir, Tamil Nadu... Tandoori dishes, curries,

RHYTHM FACTORY

ELLA DORAN

MUDCHUTE CITY FARM

and desserts with cardamom. The Goan king prawn curry or venison tikka *aflatoon* (flavored with roasted fennel, star anise and cinnamon) are recommended. Dishes £17.

The Gaucho Grill (J D2)
→ 29 Westferry Circus, E14
Tel. 020 7987 9494; Daily noon–11pm (10pm Sun)
Some may find the cowhide decor and the yuppie clientele a bit intimidating, but this Docklands branch of the small South American chain serves fantastic cuts of prime Argentinian beef, cooked on the *asado* (barbecue). Beautiful riverside location too, with a large terrace. Grill £20.

PUBS, BARS, CLUB

Dickens Inn (J A2)
→ St Katharine's Way E1
Tel. 020 7488 2208
Mon-Sat 11am–11pm;
Sun noon-10.30pm
A huge three-story, pseudo-Swiss chalet with fantastic views over the river and Tower Bridge from its broad, flowery balconies.

The Gun (J E2)
→ 27 Codharbour, E14
Tel. 020 7515 5222
Daily 10.30am–11pm

Tucked away between one of the little lanes on the Isle of Dogs and the Thames is an historic inn, where Horatio Nelson used to meet Emma Hamilton. It has a fantastic terrace overlooking the river with a surreal view of the Millennium Dome, three spacious bars and a gastro-dining area which seems to get better and better, and is often bursting at the seams with Canary Wharf workers.

Greenwich Union (J D4)
→ 56 Royal Hill, SE1
Tel. 020 8692 6258; Mon-Fri noon–11pm; Sat 11am–11pm; Sun 11.30am–11pm
With a leafy courtyard extending behind pretty cottage premises, this is a relaxed pub in which to enjoy trendy sounds, tasty snacks, and organic beer.

Rhythm Factory (J B1)
→ 16-18 Whitechapel Rd, E1
Tel. 020 7375 3774
Sun-Thu 8pm–midnight; (1am Thu); Fri 9pm–4am; Sat 10pm–7am
This dimly lit venue features more eclectic programming than many clubs: alternative rock, dubstep, punk, ska, hip-hop, etc. Room 2 here plays drum'n'bass and

can be great fun on a Saturday night.

Bethnal Green Working Men's Club (J B1)
→ 42 Pollard Row, E2
Tel. 020 7739 2727; Thu-Sun
www.workersplaytime.net
Opened in 1953 as a place for workers to relax, this club, cultural venue and party house stages all kinds of live entertainment events, with barmaids in fright wigs, water pistols and kitsch burlesque in a decor to match– crazy.

SHOPPING, ECOTOURISM

Cheshire Street (J A1)
Many independent designers have shops here.
Mar Mar Co (no. 16)
→ Tel. 020 7729 1494
Mon-Thu by appt;
Fri-Sun 11am–5pm
Scandinavian design.
Dragana Peristic (no. 34)
→ Tel. 020 7739 4484
Mon-Thu by appt;
Fri-Sun 11am–6pm
Ready-to-wear and accessories from a Serbian designer.
Ella Doran (no. 46)
→ Tel. 020 7613 0782
Mon by appt; Wed-Fri 10am–6pm; Sat-Sun noon–5pm
Tableware, roller blinds, stationery from an

acclaimed young designer.

The Laden Showroom (J A1)
→ 103 Brick Lane E1
Tel. 020 7247 2431; Mon-Sat 11am–6.30pm (7pm Sat);
Sun 10.30am–6pm
London's leading fashion store promoting, supporting and selling the work of young designers. Original styles at affordable prices: dresses, bags, shoes, jewelry – in fact everything you need from head to toe.

Butcher of Distinction (J A1)
→ 11 Dray Walk
91-95, Brick Lane, E1
Tel. 020 7770 6111
Daily 10am–7pm
Smart sportswear for men, hanging down from butcher's hooks or laid out on the marble slab.

Mudchute City Farm (J E3)
→ Pier St, Isle of Dogs, E14
Tel. 020 7515 5901
Daily 9.30am–4.30pm
Follow the path round a park laid out on former marshland to see all the farm animals. There are chickens, sheep, cows, goats, and more besides. It is an incongruous sight to see a barnyard at the foot of a skyscraper.

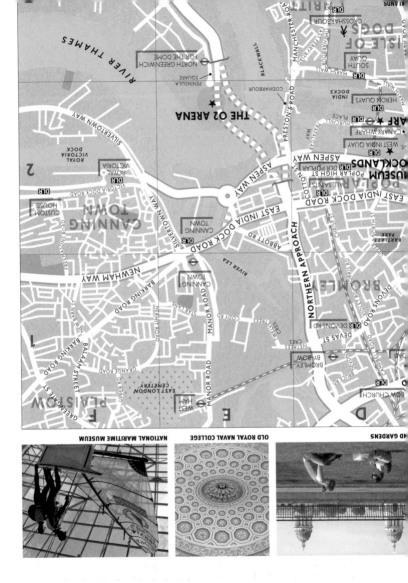

O2 ARENA

V&A MUSEUM OF CHILDHOOD

dian villa made a
al break with the
tions of Elizabethan
vagance, being a white
lelepiped decorated
a balustrade and with
ved staircase. Inside
oyal portraits, a view of
nwich by Canaletto
7–1768) and a
tiful black-and-white
floor in the Great Hall.

**d Royal
ervatory (J E4)**
eenwich Park, SE10
20 8858 4422; Daily
–5pm (8pm July-Aug)
e orders of King
es II, in 1675 Wren
an observatory in
nwich Park to 'perfect
t of navigation'.

Originally a small house, it
was enlarged by the
addition of other buildings.
In the oldest one, Flamsteed
House, is the Octagon Room
designed by Wren, while the
Meridian Building houses a
collection of astronomical
instruments including a
huge refracting telescope,
and a planetarium has laser
shows depicting the birth
and life of stars. In the north
courtyard a line represents
the official Greenwich
Meridian.

★ **Ranger's House (J E4)**
→ *Chesterfield Walk, SE10
Tel. 020 8853 0035; April-Sep:
Wed, Fri-Sun 10am–5pm; Thu
by appt; Oct-March: by appt*
This elegant redbrick

Georgian mansion (1723)
houses the collection of
diamond magnate Julius
Wernher (1850–1912): ivory,
jewelry, bronzes, porcelain
from the Middle Ages to the
18th century, and pictures
by Filippino Lippi, Memling,
De Hooch, Romney,
Reynolds and others.

★ **The O2 Arena (J E2)**
→ *Peninsula Square, SE10*
To celebrate the third
millennium, architect
Richard Rogers decided to
build the largest dome in
the world on a bend in the
river. Shaped like a flattened
egg, it is more than 3,000 ft
in circumference and
covered by a skin of one
million square ft supported

by 12 masts. Following the
scandal of its astronomical
cost (£600 million), the
former Millennium Dome
changed its name to O2 and
was relaunched as a
commercial center with a
23,000-seat arena.

★ **V&A Museum
of Childhood (J B1)**
→ *Cambridge Heath Rd, E2
Tel. 020 8983 5200
Daily 10am–5.30pm*
A glorious jumble of a
museum devoted to
childhood and housed in a
huge cast-iron hall (1851),
with rocking horses, Punch
and Judy, airplanes, and a
valuable collection of dolls'
houses from the 17th to
the 21st centuries.

AIRPORT LINKS

From Heathrow
Underground
→ *Piccadilly line; 50 mins from the airport to the city center; £4 one way*
The cheapest way.
Heathrow Express
→ *To Paddington Station in 15 mins; £14.50 one way*
The fastest way.

From Gatwick
Gatwick Express
→ *To Victoria Station in 30 mins; £17 one way*
The fastest way.

From Stansted
Stansted Express
→ *To Liverpool Street Station in 45 mins; £15 one way*
The fastest way.

ONE OF THE TWO REMAINING ROUTEMASTERS' LINES

Jesmond Dene Hotel (D C3)
→ *27 Argyle St, WC1
Tel. 020 7837 4654; www. jesmonddenehotel.co.uk*
The 25 rooms are small and spartan but clean. Friendly welcome. From £65.

The Alhambra Hotel (D C3)
→ *17-19 Argyle St, WC1
Tel. 020 7837 9575
www.alhambrahotel.com*
The rooms at the Alhambra next door are also basic but slightly more spacious, in tones of blue and cream. As its neighbor, very good value for money. From £65.

Luna & Simone Hotel (A B5)
→ *47-49 Belgrave Rd, SW1
Tel. 020 7834 5897
www.lunasimonehotel.com*
A faultless B&B with a pastel decor and 36 spacious room. The energetic and efficient staff are always on hand. From £70.

Merlyn Court Hotel (G A2)
→ *2 Barkston Gardens, SW5
Tel. 020 7370 1640
www.merlyncourthotel.com*
A quiet B&B near Earl's Court station, with ancient furniture in the pleasant rooms, which overlook a pretty square open to residents. From £75.

Brompton Hotel (G C2)
→ *30 Old Brompton Rd SW7
Tel. 020 7584 4517
www.bromhotel.com*
A small, attractive hotel close to South Kensington tube station with light and comfortable rooms, all en suite; free wi-fi and friendly staff. From £85; check their website for special offers.

Hoxton Hotel (C E1)
→ *81 Great Eastern St, EC2
Tel. 020 7550 1000
www.hoxtonhotels.com*
This 205-room 'urban lodge' was born out of Sinclair Beecham's anger at the way hotels

overcharge every service they offer. Beware though, once made, your booking won't be refundable and there's a £5 penalty if you vacate your room after the noon deadline. But, here phone calls are a few pence a minute and there is no mini bar or room service. Instead, you buy chocolate or champagne from reception, at the price you would have paid in the supermarket next door, and go next door for dinner at the Hoxton Grille. Flat screen TVs, free wi-fi, comfortable beds and luxurious duvets. From £79.

£85–100

Georgian House Hotel (A A5)
→ *35 St George's Drive, SW1
Tel. 020 7834 1438; www. georgianhousehotel.co.uk*
In an elegant 19th-century

VIA THE CHANNEL

Eurostar train
The journey is now only 2¼ hrs from Paris or Brussels, and 1¼ hrs from Lille or Calais. You arrive at St Pancras International (**D** C3), in Central London.
Information/Reservation
→ *Tel. 08705 186186 (UK) 08 92 35 35 39 (France) From €69/£59 return www.eurostar.co.uk*
From the USA
→ *Tel. 1 877 677 1066 www.britrail.com*
→ *Tel. 1 877 257 2887 www.raileurope.com/us*

Eurotunnel
Calais-Folkestone
→ *Up to four departures/hr, 24/7 (boarding time 30 mins; journey time 35 mins)*
Travel with your car via the Channel Tunnel. Arrive in Folkestone (75 miles from London). Passengers must stay with their vehicle throughout the journey.
→ *From France: take the A16 freeway, exit 42 for 'Tunnel sous la Manche / Channel Tunnel'*
Reservations
By telephone, from travel agencies, at the check-in booth in the terminal.
→ *Tel. 08705 35 35 35 www.eurotunnel.com*

Boats
The price of a return ticket depends on the length of your stay.
Norfolkline
→ *Tel. 0870 870 1020 www.norfolkline-ferries. co.uk*
A 1¾-hour crossing from Dunkirk to Dover; from €20/person with bike; €30/person with car.

AIRPORTS

Heathrow and Gatwick the two largest of London's five international airports.

Heathrow Airport
→ Tel. 08700 000 123
www.heathrowairport.com

Gatwick Airport
→ Tel. 08700 002 468
www.gatwickairport.co.uk

City Airport
→ Tel. 020 7646 0088
www.londoncityairport.com

Stansted Airport
→ Tel. 08700 000 303
www.stanstedairport.com

Luton Airport
→ Tel. 01582 405 100
www.london-luton.co.uk

AIRPORTS

Finding a cheap, clean and comfortable hotel in London is a challenge. Hotels in the UK's capital city are also, given their high prices, often less comfortable than in most other European capitals.

• Unless otherwise indicated, the prices listed here are per night for a double room en suite, off season, VAT and breakfast included.

• If you are paying by bank card, most B&Bs will charge an extra 3–5 percent.

• It is often cheaper to book via the hotel's website.

B&Bs

Below are two of the many companies based in London that could help you find a B & B in the capital.

Uptown Reservations
→ Tel. +44 (0) 20 7937 2001
Fax + 44 (0) 20 7937 6660
www.uptownres.co.uk
From £80 per night per room for a single traveler;

from £105 per night per double or twin room. There is a £5 supplement per room for a one-night stay.

The London Bed & Breakfast Agency
→ Tel. (+44) 20 7586 2768
www.londonbb.com
From £37 per person per night for two sharing, with en-suite (from £50 for a single traveler). Two-night stay minimum.

YOUTH HOSTEL

You must be a member of the International Federation of Youth Hostels to stay in state-run youth hostels. You can join on arrival (£16; under 26 yrs, £10).

London YHA
→ www.yha.org.uk
London St Pauls (C B3)
→ 36 Carter Lane, EC4
London St Pancras (D C3)
→ 79-81 Euston Rd, NW1
London Oxford St (B B3)
→ 14 Noel Street W1

London Earl's Court (G A3)
→ 38 Bolton Gardens SW5
Generator (D C4)
→ Compton Place WC1
Tel. 020 7388 7666
www.generatorhostels.com
An unusual youth hostel in an old police station. Ultramodern decor and the benefits of a central location. Bar and nightly events. Dormitories and double, triple rooms. From £20/pers.

UNIVERSITY HALL OF RESIDENCE

Queen Alexandra's House (G B1)
→ Bremner Rd, Kensington Gore, SW7; Tel. 020 7589 1120
Near the Royal Albert Hall, this women's hall of residence is in an extraordinary building, and open to female non-students during the summer term (April to mid-July). Single rooms only.

£30 per night, breakfast and dinner included.

£60–85

Marble Arch Inn (E B4)
→ 49-50 Upper Berkeley St, W1; Tel. 020 7723 7888
www.marblearch-inn.co.uk
One of the cheapest hotels to be found in the city, and little more than a stone's throw from Hyde Park. Comfortable rooms with small en-suite bathrooms and continental breakfast. From £45.

Cherry Court Hotel (A A5)
→ 23 Hugh St, SW1
Tel. 020 7828 2840
www.cherrycourthotel.co.uk
A small B&B in a five-story Victorian house, with 12 tiny but tastefully decorated rooms, with en-suite shower or bathroom. A rudimentary breakfast is served in the rooms. Free Internet access. £60.

Transportation in London

Bakerloo	Hammersmith & City	Victoria
Central	Jubilee	Waterloo & City
Circle	Metropolitan	Overground
District	Northern	DLR
East London	Piccadilly	

line closed, replacement bus services operate

under construction

© Transport for London

Reg. user No. 08/1154/P

MAYOR OF LONDON

Website
tfl.gov.uk

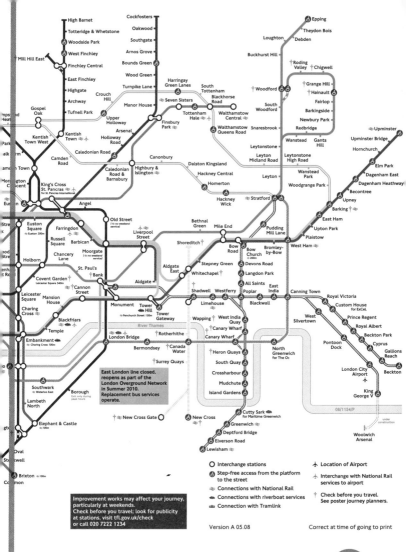

Cockfosters
High Barnet
Totteridge & Whetstone
Woodside Park
West Finchley
Mill Hill East
Finchley Central
East Finchley
Highgate
Archway
Tufnell Park
Oakwood
Southgate
Arnos Grove
Bounds Green
Wood Green
Turnpike Lane
Harringay Green Lanes
Crouch Hill
Manor House
Upper Holloway
Finsbury Park
Arsenal
Holloway Road
Caledonian Road
Camden Road
Caledonian Road & Barnsbury
Highbury & Islington
Canonbury
Dalston Kingsland
Hackney Central
Homerton
Hackney Wick
Stratford
Epping
Theydon Bois
Debden
Loughton
Buckhurst Hill
Roding Valley
Chigwell
Grange Hill
Hainault
Fairlop
Barkingside
Newbury Park
Redbridge
Wanstead
Gants Hill
Woodford
South Woodford
Snaresbrook
Leytonstone
Leytonstone High Road
Leyton Midland Road
Leyton
Wanstead Park
Woodgrange Park
South Tottenham
Blackhorse Road
Tottenham Hale
Walthamstow Central
Walthamstow Queens Road
Harringay
Seven Sisters
Upminster
Upminster Bridge
Hornchurch
Elm Park
Dagenham East
Dagenham Heathway
Becontree
Upney
Barking
East Ham
Upton Park
Plaistow
West Ham
Gospel Oak
Kentish Town West
Kentish Town
Camden Town
Mornington Crescent
King's Cross St. Pancras
for St. Pancras International
Euston
Angel
Euston Square
Farringdon
Russell Square
Barbican
Old Street
no weekend service
Liverpool Street
Moorgate
no weekend service
Holborn
Chancery Lane
St. Paul's
Bank
Bethnal Green
Mile End
Shoreditch †
Stepney Green
Whitechapel
Aldgate East
Aldgate
Bow Road
Bow Church
Devons Road
Langdon Park
All Saints
Poplar
Bromley-by-Bow
Pudding Mill Lane
Covent Garden
Leicester Square 340m
Leicester Square
Charing Cross
Mansion House
Cannon Street
Monument
Tower Hill
Penchurch Street 130m
Tower Gateway
West India Quay
Canary Wharf
Canary Wharf
Heron Quays
South Quay
Crossharbour
Mudchute
Island Gardens
Shadwell
Westferry
Limehouse
Wapping
Rotherhithe
Bermondsey
Canada Water
Surrey Quays
West India Quay
East India
Canning Town
Blackwall
North Greenwich
for The O2
Royal Victoria
Custom House
for ExCeL
Prince Regent
Royal Albert
Beckton Park
Cyprus
Gallions Reach
Beckton
West Silvertown
Pontoon Dock
London City Airport
King George V
Woolwich Arsenal
under construction
Blackfriars
Temple
Embankment
Charing Cross 100m
London Bridge
River Thames
Southwark
Waterloo East
Borough
Exit only during peak hours
Lambeth North
Elephant & Castle
100m
Oval
Stockwell
Brixton 100m
Clapham Common
New Cross Gate
New Cross
Cutty Sark
for Maritime Greenwich
Greenwich
Deptford Bridge
Elverson Road
Lewisham
08/1154/P

East London line closed, reopens as part of the London Overground Network in Summer 2010. Replacement bus services operate.

○ Interchange stations
● Step-free access from the platform to the street
⇌ Connections with National Rail
⛴ Connections with riverboat services
🚋 Connection with Tramlink

✈ Location of Airport
✈ Interchange with National Rail services to airport
† Check before you travel. See poster journey planners.

Version A 05.08

Correct at time of going to print

Improvement works may affect your journey, particularly at weekends.
Check before you travel; look for publicity at stations, visit tfl.gov.uk/check or call 020 7222 1234

24 hour travel information
020 7222 1234

Transport for London

UNDERGROUND

NDON AND ITS RAILWAY STATIONS

Information
→ Tel. 020 7222 1234
www.tfl.gov.uk
Six zones. Zones 1 and 2
cover Central London.
Subway and DLR
→ Mon-Sat 5.30am–
12.30am; Sun 7.30am–
11.30pm
Subway (or 'Tube')
12 lines. Some stations
close at weekends and
during off-peak periods.
Docklands Light Railway
The DLR links the City to
the Docklands and East
End; under expansion.
Tickets
→ £4 single (zones 1-2)
Bus
→ Daily 5am–midnight
Check the destination
displayed on the front
(some buses do not run
the full length of the
line).
Night buses
→ Until 5am on some lines
Most go by Trafalgar
Square.
Tickets
→ £2 single; bus pass
£3.50 (one day)
In central London you
must buy tickets before
you board the bus from a
machine at a bus stop.
Oyster Card
→ From subway stations;
£3 deposit, then £1–2 per
journey with a daily max.
cap of £6.30
Subway and bus pass
which you validate upon
entering and leaving the
station.
London Travelcard
Bus, subway, trains
(within London).
→ £6.80/one day;
£17.40/three days; £24.20/
one week (zones 1-2)

e second, newly built,
next to King's Cross
Pancras and therefore
ry convenient for
avelers using the new
rostar terminal.
acious, modern rooms.
eakfast £7.

**indermere
otel (A** A5)
142-144 Warwick Way, SW1
l. 020 7834 5163
ww.windermere-hotel.co.uk
award-winning B & B
a Victorian building
ry close to Victoria
ation, it has a labyrinth of
aircases and comfortable
oms. Good restaurant.
ry good, copious
eakfast. From £114.

UXURY HOTELS

you are not staying at
ese hotels why not go there
afternoon tea or evening
inks?

avoy Hotel (B E4)
Strand, WC2

Tel. 020 7836 4343
www.fairmont.com/Savoy
This grand hotel (1889)
with marble lobby and
Art Deco influence in the
rooms will reopen in May
2009 after a two-year,
£100 million renovation.
Afternoon tea.
Claridge's (E D4)
→ Brook St, W1
Tel. 020 7629 8860
www.maybourne.com
An Art Deco gem in Mayfair,
it started life as a small
hotel in 1812. Afternoon tea
3–5.30pm (reserve): £31,
champagne tea £40. £320.
The Ritz (A A1)
→ 150 Piccadilly W1
Tel. 020 7493 8181
www.theritzlondon.com
World-famous luxury hotel
built in 1898 in Louis XIV
style. From £320. Book
at least four weeks ahead
for afternoon tea (five
sittings a day, £36).
Brown's Hotel (F D5)
→ Albemarle St, W1

Tel. 020 7493 6020
www.brownshotel.com
The historic Brown's was
established in 1837 by
Byron's valet. It became
part of Rocco Forte's
empire in 2003,
refurbished and decorated
with style and elegance by
Olga Polizzi. From £310;
breakfast £20. You could
also drop by for afternoon
tea at the English Tea Room
(3–6pm, £29.50) or for
cocktails at the Donovan.
**Mandarin Oriental
Hyde Park (G** E1)
→ 66 Knightsbridge SW1
Tel. 020 7235 2000
www.mandarinoriental.com
Right on Hyde Park, this is
one of London's grandest
hotels, in expensively
and impeccably renovated
Edwardian style, with lots
of marble. It also has one
of London's trendiest bars
and definitely the best spa
(open to non guests)
in the country. From £285.

TAXIS

Black cabs
If the sign on the roof is illuminated, the taxi is unoccupied. Tell the driver where you want to go before getting in.
→ *Pick-up charge £2.20 then about £1.50/mile*

Minicabs
Self-employed drivers. Always call a licensed company and fix the price for your journey beforehand.

Cabwise
→ *Text 'HOME' to 60835 wherever you are in London to receive two names of local licensed companies*

Addison Lee
→ *Tel. 020 7387 8888*

ST PANCRAS INTERNATIONAL

DLR IN CANARY WHARF

TRAIN STATIONS

Information
→ *Tel. 08457 48 49 50*
Charing Cross (H A2)
→ *Canterbury, southeast*
Euston (D B4)
→ *Glasgow, Liverpool, north, northwest*
St Pancras International / King's Cross (D C3)
→ *Edinburgh, Cambridge, north, northeast*
Liverpool Street (C D2)
→ *Cambridge, east coast*
Paddington (F E1)
→ *Bath, Oxford, Statford-upon-Avon, southwest, west*
Victoria (A A4)
→ *Brighton, southwest*
Waterloo (H C3)
→ *Dover, south, southwest*

house a few minutes' walk from Victoria Station, this cozy B&B is worth a mention for its attractive internet special offers. Full English breakfast. £89.

Hampstead Village Guesthouse (off **D** A2)
→ *2 Kemplay Rd, NW3 Hampstead subway station Tel. 020 7435 8679; www. hampsteadguesthouse.com*
A B&B in the prettiest street, with nine rooms full of character (one has a free-standing bath tub, another has its own tiny terrace), well-lit and filled with books and antiques unearthed by the owners in markets and second-hand stores. Lovely garden where breakfast is served in summer. From £90. Breakfast £7.

Vicarage Hotel (**F** D3)
→ *10 Vicarage Gate W8 Tel. 020 7229 4030; www. londonvicaragehotel.com*
This beautiful B&B is in a fine Victorian house at the heart of Kensington's residential district. Some of the rooms are very big, with large mirrors and furniture made of fine wood. Friendly staff. From £78.

Jenkin's Hotel (**D** C4)
→ *45 Cartwright Gardens, WC1; Tel. 020 7387 2067 www.jenkinshotel. demon.co.uk*
This hotel stands in a lovely crescent-shaped street built at the turn of the 19th century and has been a hotel since the 1920s. It is, however, extremely well preserved, with 14 small, well-equipped rooms. Guests have access to a tennis court. From £89.

Winchester Hotel (**A** A5)
→ *17 Belgrave Rd. SW1 Tel. 020 7828 2972 www.winchester-hotel.net*
An elegant B&B with large mirrors, basins of flowers, beautiful wall fabrics and spacious rooms. From £89.

La Gaffe (off **D** A1)
→ *107-111 Heath St, NW3 Tel. 020 7435 8965 (Hampstead subway station) www.lagaffe.co.uk*
Eighteen comfortable rooms, some with four-poster beds, all with flowery bedspreads and curtains. Yes, they are small but you are at the heart of the beautiful Hampstead 'village' and a few minutes's walk from the Heath. Patio and terrace. From £95.

Amsterdam (off **G** A2)
→ *7 Trebovir Rd, SW5 Tel. 020 7370 5084 (Earl's Court subway station)*
A 'three-star hotel with a five-star attitude', it is indeed a very cozy B&B, with a tranquil atmosphere and views over the shady private garden from some of the rooms. From £98.

Morgan Hotel (**B** B2)
→ *24 Bloomsbury St, WC1 Tel. 020 7636 3735*

www.morganhotel.co.uk
Housed in a Georgian house so typical of the Bloomsbury area, the Morgan is a friendly family-run hotel very well situated next to the British Museum. Most rooms are small but well appointed and clean; no elevator. From £98.

Premier Inn London – County Hall (**E** B3)
→ *2 County Hall Building Belvedere Rd, SE1 Tel. 0870 230 3300*
Premier Inn London – King's Cross (**D** D3)
→ *York Way Tel. 0870 990 6414 www.premiertravelinn.co.uk*
The Premier Inns hotels are excellent value for money, especially for families or small groups as some rooms sleep up to four people for £99 per room. The first is a modern hotel at the back of County Hall (no views of the Thames);

The names of streets, monuments and places to visit are listed alphabetically. They are followed by one or several map references (**F** A3), whose first letter in bold refers to the corresponding area and map.